November 2015
To Brother :
May All Your Facilitations

FACILITATING FATHERS' GROUPS

22 Keys to Group Mastery

HAJI SHEARER

Be Successful,

Love,

P & S Press
Boston, Massachusetts

Copyright © 2014 Haji Shearer

ISBN: 098950090X

ISBN-13: 9780989500906

P & S Press

Published in the United States by P & S Press

Library of Congress Cataloguing-in-Publication Data

Shearer, Haji 1962-

Facilitating Fathers' Groups: 22 Keys to Group Mastery/ Haji Shearer

p. cm.

1. Social Work. 2. Fatherhood. 3. Group Dynamics. 4. Leadership. I. Title.

Printed in the United States of America

Cover and back photos: Craig Bailey, Perspective Photo

Haji Shearer photo: Alinda Asiam Bostick, Asiam Design Photography

Editing by: Mary C. Lewis, MCL Editing, Etc.

Copies of *Facilitating Fathers' Groups* may be ordered at: www.hajishearer.com

10 9 8 7 6 5 4 3 2 1

First Edition

Here's What People Are Saying About
Facilitating Fathers' Groups:
22 Keys to Group Mastery

Facilitating Fathers' Groups: 22 Keys to Group Mastery is a long awaited instruction manual to change the outlook of families and communities. This book will help us in this industry to turn ordinary men into agents for change. I have been in a session with Hajj and have seen how great he facilitates. He is as defined and as strong as this long awaited manual for change.

—**Joel Austin**, President/CEO of Daddy University Inc., Founder of the National Fatherhood Conference, The Tri-State Daddy Daughter Dance, and Chief Facilitator of the Fathers Club group.

Facilitating Father's Groups is a game-changer...an indispensable resource for any individual or organization working with dads or men. Haji Shearer has succeeded on two fronts: creating a comprehensive framework for understanding the complexity of successful group facilitation and writing a practical, nuts & bolts guide for the novice and seasoned practitioner alike. Just like his speaking and teaching, Haji has now put the same contagious energy, utter clarity, and actionable insight to paper. The result is a true contribution to the fields of fatherhood, parenting, social work and psychology.

—**John Badalament**, Program Director of The Fatherhood Project at Massachusetts General Hospital and author of *The Modern Dad's Dilemma: How To Stay Connected With Your Kids In A Rapidly Changing World*

I can't say enough about my good friend Haji and his work in the fatherhood movement. It brings me joy to have read this awesome work that eloquently captures a solution to the epidemic of fatherlessness, one of the most serious problems we face in our society today. Haji has developed the ideas in this book based on his commitment and years of successfully facilitating groups and supporting dads and families. This book highlights and reinforces the fierce Urgency of Now! We need all hands on deck to solve this epidemic and the book you hold will help you take many steps in the right direction.

—**Kenneth Braswell, Sr.**, Executive Director, Fathers Incorporated; Director, National Responsible Fatherhood Clearinghouse and author of *When the Tear Won't Fall: One Man's Journey through the Intimate Struggles of Manhood and Fatherhood*

Haji has incorporated his background and expertise as a facilitator and father to develop *Facilitating Fathers' Groups: 22 Keys to Group Mastery*, a comprehensive set of discussions and activities that will reinforce the idea that the job of parenting; teaching, protecting, nurturing children, is one of the most important responsibilities an adult can assume. Parents need a variety of resources to help them prepare for and cope with the demands and challenges of family life. Preparing group facilitators to engage men, not just as men but as fathers is a major step in supporting the concept that "Dads are parent too."

—**Richard Claytor**, Member, Board of Directors Fathers and Families Coalition of America

I believe Haji was born to facilitate and to write this road map for those of us who would follow. It is a life's work birthed out of raw struggle and much love. *Facilitating Fathers' Groups: 22 Keys to Group Mastery* is a must have for professionals in the field or anyone who is really looking to communicate better and do mind blowing group work. Haji, thank you for providing us with street lights.

—**Len Hayes**, Independent Fathers' Group Facilitator

Haji Shearer has been a powerful and active force in not only the fatherhood movement but the family empowerment movement as well. His book, *Facilitating Fathers' Groups*, gives you everything you need to successfully facilitate groups that speak to the needs and concerns of fathers. Once you absorb the wisdom contained in these pages, you'll be ready and able to provide a safe and sacred space where fathers can celebrate their successes, enhance their skills as parents and guide their children towards lifelong success. Before you even finish *Facilitating Fathers' Groups*, you'll be equipped and inspired to engage fathers in a way that demonstrates respect, collaborative exchange and understanding. Read this book and transform the way you communicate and work with fathers.

—**Cassandra Mack**, CEO, Strategies for Empowered Living and author of *The Single Mom's Little Book of Wisdom*

Haji Shearer is a gift to all of us who work with men and fathers. He invites us to become masters through understanding our strengths and developing our gifts. Whether it's the barrio, the hood, or the suburb, he has wisdom, soul, and experience to offer. He offers an amazing depth of knowledge and an open heart, and the capacity to share it with excitement and joy. I will reread this book many times. Every time I put it down I carry new thoughts and ideas into practice—a boost for creativity and greater connection with men and groups. I cannot think of a friend who will not benefit from a copy of this gem. You will too!

—**Fernando Mederos**, Board Co-Chair National Latino Alliance for the Elimination of Domestic Violence

Men have a deep reservoir for creating—and sustaining—loving relationships. Sadly, mainstream culture often undermines our efforts. So it is up to us—men and others who have worked with men and fathers in groups—to pick up the slack. We know firsthand the power found in a circle of men helping one another. It is among the most moving forces for positive change—from stirring our hearts to fostering peace in our homes and our communities. Haji Shearer has captured that loving power in a new book that does more than open the door into the realm of men's personal growth. He has created a guide so that once inside we can access men's innate capacity to love, to nurture and grow. In a world in need of more openhearted men this book is a boundless gift.

—**Rob Okun**, editor of Voice Male magazine and the forthcoming book, *VOICE MALE: The Untold Story of the Profeminist Men's Movement*

Haji Shearer is a Master Facilitator and Trainer. As one of the leaders of the Fatherhood Movement in New England, his work has touched many people and positively influenced many lives. With his book, *Facilitating Fathers' Groups: 22 Keys to Group Mastery*, Mr. Shearer proves that he is also a brilliant writer and gifted teacher. I consider this book my own personal classroom. I've never been formally trained in group facilitation, so this book has been a Godsend for me. It has helped to broaden my understanding of group dynamics and is guiding me in developing a more effective facilitation style. Whether you're a beginner or an experienced facilitator, this book can help you as it has helped me.

—**John O'Neil**, Family Nurturing Center of Massachusetts, Fathers' Program Director

I am very excited about this book! It is the "missing link" in our young but growing field of group-based fatherhood skills education. Haji

Shearer has succeeded in making the art and science of effective group facilitation clear, accessible, and fun. *Facilitating Father's Groups* is a significant contribution to the field, and I will be recommending it as a companion to my curriculum.

—**Mark Perlman**, Author/Trainer, *The Nurturing Father's Program*

Haji Shearer has long been an active figure in the fatherhood movement—from Boston to the White House—working tirelessly across the lines of race, class, and gender, improving the lives of children and mothers by educating, empowering, and healing fathers. *Facilitating Fathers' Groups: 22 Keys to Group Mastery* is both witty and wise; more importantly, it is *practical.* We ask with increasing urgency *How do we help construct a healthy, new, nurturing masculinity?* Start by reading this book.

—**Donald N.S. Unger**, PhD, author of *Men* Can: *The Changing Image & Reality of Fatherhood in America*

Facilitating Fathers' Groups is essential reading for all fatherhood practitioners, particularly those working with dads in groups, but also program managers and others who play key roles in helping fathers navigate their journey to be the best dad they can for their kids. I've been doing work with fathers and fatherhood programs since 1988 and this is one of the most readable and useful books I've come across in that time. Enjoy!

—**Nigel Vann**, Senior Technical Specialist, ICF International, and long-time consultant to fatherhood programs

Facilitating Fathers' Groups: 22 Keys To Group Mastery is a masterful work and a must read for anyone wanting to run a successful fathers group! Written by an expert in his field, Haji's genuine passion for helping fathers is noble and downright infectious. The insight he shares will equip the reader with the essential tools needed to help fathers see the value in authentic fatherhood and reach their potential as dads. The wisdom revealed here will impact many future generations of fathers and help to break the vicious cycle of fatherlessness in our country. Bravo, bravo, bravo!

—**Zoro**, World-renowned drummer for Lenny Kravitz, Bobby Brown, Frankie Valli and the Four Seasons and author of *The Big Gig: Big-Picture Thinking For Success*

Dedication

To God, who wakes me up.
To Mom, who instilled a love of letters.
To Dad, who held it down.

Table of Contents

Author's Note

All the fathers described herein are composites. Identifying characteristics of all the men and family members mentioned have been mixed and changed to maintain the confidentiality of group members.

Introduction

It's a great time to be a father!

Parenting has been the primary responsibility of women for most of recent history. In the last 30 years a new world has opened up for men as we are welcome not only at the conception, but also more and more at the birth and subsequent upbringing of the next generation. As many fathers became involved in raising our children we realized what mothers have always known. Children are amazing! Men who are involved fathers report higher overall satisfaction in their own lives, not to mention the myriad benefits that an involved father brings to his children.[1]

Unfortunately, many families are not partaking in this cornucopia of benefits. According to the U.S. Census of 2009, 45

1 Allen, S., & K. Daley (May 2007). *The Effects of Father Involvement: An Updated Research Summary of the Evidence*, Guelph, Ontario: Centre for Families, Work & Well-Being. http://fira.ca/cms/documents/29/Effects_of_Father_Involvement.pdf.

Amato, P. R., & Rivera, F. (1999). Paternal Involvement and Children's Behavior Problems. *Journal of Marriage and the Family, 61,* 375–384.

Harrington, B., F. Van Deusen, & B. Humberd (2011). *The New Dad: Caring, Committed and Conflicted.* Boston: Boston College Center for Work & Family. http://www.bc.edu/content/dam/files/centers/cwf/pdf/FH-Study-Web-2.pdf.

Nord, Christine Winquist (April 1998). Issue Brief: Students Do Better When Their Fathers Are Involved at School. Washington, DC: Department of Education, Office of Educational Research and Improvement, National Center for Education Statistics. http://nces.ed.gov/pubs98/98121.pdf.

percent of Black children (ages 6 to 11) grow up in single-parent homes which are predominately led by mothers only. The rate is 17 percent in Latino families, 14 percent for White families and 7 percent for Asian families.[2] Those numbers represent pain and shame for millions of boys and girls, men and women. I've sat with emotionally armored, urban men, adults with their own families, who cried uncontrollably when given some quiet time to reflect on the loss of their own fathers.

In order to lower these incidences of father absence, to decrease the pain in homes across the country and across the globe, to help fathers stay connected with their families and aware of the joy and the pain that being a parent entails, in order to take on these and other family building initiatives, we must change the way we support men as parents. We must create fun, educational environments that encourage men to become and remain fathers and dads, especially in communities where father absence is most serious. Groups of men gathered together, in a structured format, with the express purpose of supporting one another to become more involved, loving fathers is an idea whose time has come. *Facilitating Fathers' Groups: 22 Keys to Group Mastery* will explain how, with the help of a high quality fathering curriculum you can take that notion from idea to reality.

A lot of social science research demonstrates how fathers help to improve outcomes for children when they are involved in responsible, compassionate interactions with the family. Increases in self-esteem, behavior, academics, participation in athletics and, of course, income have all been attributed to having a father present. There's less science about how to get a dad to that place where having responsible, compassionate interactions with his family is

2 http://www.census.gov/prod/2009pubs/p20-561.pdf

the norm. In this book, you will read examples of men who modified their behavior based on requests from their own sense of a higher purpose, as well as from their co-parent and children.

I recall the mom who encouraged her husband to attend one of our 13-session programs. When she attended the graduation she came up to me solo and said, "I don't know what you did, but he changed. He spends more time with the kids. He helps me around the house more. He's just easier to be around. Thank you."

The amazing thing about our private conversation is I knew from sitting in the group with her husband and eight other men that doing these additional things around the house was not, in his view, separate from *his* self-interest. He *wanted* to do the extra tasks because he wanted to be a good father and husband. It was simply that when he and his wife started arguing about the family, tensions got high, positions became rigid and egos got involved. Having a group of men around him—other fathers—he could discuss the same issues without the intense charge that occurred when he and his wife were arguing. A fathers' group allowed him to see the dynamic from a higher perspective.

When I first started to facilitate groups for fathers in 1999, many people in the human services industry told me men would not come to groups. Support groups focused on parenting education had been growing in popularity for a couple of decades, but that phrase was really understood to mean support groups focused on mothering education. I had worked with fathers on a one-to-one basis for years regarding being more engaged as a parent and had done some of my own personal development work in groups, so I *knew* men would enjoy this kind of experience if it was offered to them in a high quality, welcoming manner.

What I've been blessed to see for myself and scores of other group facilitators, is that 10 to 15 men at a time will voluntarily agree to start a group, and only two or three of them drop out. I'm convinced that most men who are fathers, or in the role of fathers, will participate in a well-run group when given the opportunity. And the changes that then take place in that father's family are profound!

In order for these profound changes to reach more families, more facilitators will need to run high quality groups. There are several good fatherhood curricula on the market. The one I use most often is *The Nurturing Father's Program* by Mark Perlman (Sarasota: Center for Growth & Development, 2008). It takes several cycles to become proficient in the multidimensional experience of facilitating a well-run group. That's where *Facilitating Fathers' Groups* comes in. You can use any good curriculum on the market or develop your own, and this book will provide insights and techniques that will allow you to become a master facilitator in less time.

No book can replace interactive, in-person trainings, or help you learn the overall flow of a specific curriculum you may use. However, the book you are holding will help you to grasp the subtleties of managing group dynamics. There are scores of websites you can visit that will help you understand the basic stages of group process (forming, storming, norming, performing and adjourning), but *Facilitating Fathers' Groups: 22 Keys to Group Mastery* will give you much more. In exploring the 22 archetypes that you as a facilitator can try on and learn to use at appropriate times in the lifespan of a group, you will develop the resources necessary to guide your group to the highest level of functioning in the shortest amount of time and make the group experience more pleasurable for you and the participants.

This book will explain not only what to *do* as a facilitator, but also how to *be*. It's the facilitation guide that you can keep throughout your career to both troubleshoot specific problems that come up in groups and foreshadow situations that have yet to occur in your practice. That's because of this book's primary driving feature—facilitator archetypes. Archetypes are present in all cultures to symbolize certain states of consciousness. I've modernized 22 archetypes from a centuries-old personality grid to represent characters that are familiar to everyone and present, in some degree, in all our thoughts. Then I've identified how these archetypes can be helpful in facilitating an extraordinary group experience.

The title of the book and the examples in each chapter exclusively reflect my work with fathers' groups. However, it will be obvious to any interested facilitator that these archetypes and the book can be effectively applied to any type of facilitation work. I've personally used these techniques to facilitate business meetings, family meetings and couples groups, but I decided to dig deep in the niche of male parenting groups because that is such a neglected population in which the necessity for well-run groups needs to be highlighted.

By becoming familiar with the material presented in *Facilitating Fathers' Groups* a facilitator will be able to better understand and appreciate the multidimensional nature of group work. One of the most exciting and unruly things about group work is so many things are going simultaneously. A great facilitator is able to remain aware of all that energy without tamping it down. The reality is a facilitator must present different faces to the group at different times.

What I'm describing is far more subtle than simply the "good cop" facilitator and the "bad cop" facilitator. The facilitator has a separate relationship with every person in the group and has a relationship with the entire group as a whole. Different personalities require different inputs to grow and the facilitator has to be aware of that. And that's just at a conscious level; on a subconscious level, thoughts and games and agendas are being played out that can torpedo a group if the leader is not watching out for it.

Facilitating Fathers' Groups will open the facilitator's eyes to the complex dynamic he shepherds the men through and provide the reader with an abundance of methods to promote individual growth and group cohesion. The challenge of blending the multiple personalities of group participants into a healthy whole can be accomplished by a facilitator whose thoughts are expansive enough to incorporate the heart of each father in the room. *Facilitating Fathers' Groups* will illustrate a path that combines all the group members' personalities into a functioning whole.

As a group facilitator you will enjoy returning to *Facilitating Fathers' Groups* again and again. The complexities of the archetypes described in each chapter are worthy of ongoing reflection and study. In fact, *Facilitating Fathers' Groups* is not a book you must read from start to finish. Every facilitator will have archetypes that attract him and archetypes that repel him. It's normal to want to immediately start reading those chapters. It's okay, go ahead.

Feel free to make index cards of your favorite and least favorite archetypes and their qualities. Reflecting on why you are drawn to certain characters and repulsed by others will certainly shed light on your own personality. Recognizing that no single archetype is the best to lead a group at all times may be the most valuable lesson that *Facilitating Fathers' Groups* brings you.

This book can be used alongside a good fatherhood curriculum. It is not meant to replace an activity-based guide for running groups. Think of your curriculum as a bus. As the facilitator you are the driver. The participants are passengers. An excellent driver wears many hats. He knows how to welcome people on board at the start of a journey, keeps an eye on passengers to make sure all is well, knows how to intervene if passengers behave dangerously and continually scans the dashboard gauges to make sure operating systems and fuel are good. He does all this while keeping his eyes on the road. The excellent driver avoids obstacles, knows landmarks along the route and keeps the temperature steady.

Another benefit of using this book is that facilitators can discuss archetypes with other facilitators and give examples of when they were used and when participants brought them up. The 22 archetypes are fundamental to all people who facilitate groups yet they are not readily discussed as a framework for understanding how to make groups work better, and here is a huge benefit of reading the book. Not only can you use the archetypes to make your groups function better, it's an easy system to initiate conversations with other facilitators about group dynamics. Be the first one in your community or at a conference to talk about The Salesman and The CEO and The Recluse. Facilitators will understand that you are giving names to concepts they have been experimenting with already. It's like you're the guy who gets everyone to agree that thing you sit on is going to be called "chair" and now we can talk about some of the particulars of when and how to use it.

I wrote this book to both deepen and elevate the discussion about facilitating groups for men. With the number of absent fathers, community violence, family drama, substance use and other symptoms of personal pain in men, I am enthusiastic about spreading a message that allows men to alleviate their pain and achieve a level of healing in a setting that's more comfortable for most men than individual therapy. Individual psychotherapy for men, especially for men of color, is not usually high on our priority list. However, working in a group with other men takes away some of the sigma of "asking for help" or admitting "something is wrong with me" and universalizes the need for human beings, female or male, to connect with one another in a supportive environment.

When I realized I wanted to capture the magic and miracles of a well-run fathers' group in a book format that would inspire and guide people to duplicate the practice on their own, I struggled with how to format it. There were so many layers and angles that I would have to cover, and the thought of addressing the process in straight linear fashion seemed not only daunting, but somehow inaccurate. Then one day after I finished meditating the thought hit me: use the 22 Major Arcana from the Tarot Deck. As a young man I had used the 78 cards of the Tarot as a personal discovery tool and found them uncannily accurate in terms of understanding situations and phenomena that were happening in my life. Eventually, my intuition grew strong enough that I had a sense of what the Tarot cards would tell me before I used them and thus my motivation to use the cards waned.

I very rarely pulled out either of the decks I still owned, but it was immediately obvious to me that the 22 characters in the primary Tarot story would be perfect to hang my exploration of group dynamics on (there are another 56 characters who play a supporting role for the 78 cards overall). The 22 characters represent archetypes that are largely universal, but I modernized some and shaped them to better reflect the needs of a group facilitator. Those 22 chapters became scaffolding that I could reasonably build my book around.

The book reflects the holographic nature of the Tarot. Each archetype can stand on its own; plus by divining any single image deeply enough, you can see into all the archetypes through any individual one. This means it is possible to pick up the book anywhere and start to read. Just by perusing the archetypes' names in the Table of Contents, you probably will want to go to specific chapters, either because you closely identify with an archetype or you feel repulsed by a particular archetype. Any strong feelings about these symbolic representations should alert you to a sympathetic resonance of identity or deeply rooted repulsion. On the other hand, you probably have as much, if not more, to learn from the archetypes to which you do not feel a strong repulsion or attraction .so you will definitely want to read about each archetype in order to fully round out your facilitation skills.

In order to help you get a complete picture of the archetypes, each chapter opens with an Affirmation that illuminates the outcome that the archetype provided for the group. This is followed by a detailed description of the archetype that shows how the characteristics can best be used when facilitating. To give a clearer picture of possible uses of the character, I have included an Example of how I have seen, first, a facilitator use the archetype, and then, how I have seen a participant use it. It's helpful to know how participants use various archetypes and which ones they are more drawn to because this gives you more insight into who that father is. These sections of chapters can be thought of as a bit of a personality inventory.

Next up in each chapter is a brief examination of the Shadow aspect of the archetype. All the archetypes are positive if used at the right time, in the right manner. But just as even healthy foods can be harmful if taken in excess or prepared incorrectly so, too, can a beneficial archetype turn negative if it is misused in service. The Shadow section will alert you to how each seemingly benign manifestation can turn sour if you don't tend it with care. The Shadow section gives you some ideas to recognize if you are operating your archetype under the influence of ego—which is definitely a turnoff. The breakout prominence of the Shadow of each archetype is also meant to normalize it. You will deal with the Shadow elements because the group is about healing the facilitator as well as the participants. Acknowledging the Shadow when he appears is necessary to overcome its negative influences.

The Shadow is followed by Recommendations. I provide two or three simplified, practical tips for implementing the powers of each archetype. Each chapter closes with a Power Question you can ask yourself that will start generating some healthy thoughts about how you can use the skill. Too often we ask ourselves questions in a way that presupposes a negative answer, like, "Why is my life so fouled up?" Since your brain wants to supply you with answers, it comes up with reasons why your life is so fouled up. Instead, if you ask what is working in my life, you will get answers that acknowledge your successes. The Power Question is meant to get you thinking in a way that focuses on the useful building materials you have within and around you.

The uniform presentation of each chapter will remove some barriers to thinking about the archetypes which are all stored in our collective unconscious, but you may not have given any serious thought to some of them for a long time. It also makes it easy for you to flip through chapters to compare Affirmations, Recommendations, Power Questions or longer sections.

Ultimately, this book will make it easier for you to create spaces that honor the masculine in family life. By encouraging men to be more involved, nurturing fathers, you are helping to build stronger families and communities. Yes, it's a great time to be a father and with *Facilitating Fathers' Groups: 22 Keys to Group Mastery,* you can open the door for more men to participate in one of the best experiences on the planet.

May Your Facilitation Create Peace in Our World.

1 The Salesman

Affirmation

My groups are a valuable service.

Description

As The Salesman, you are enthusiastic. Your energy is contagious. You're passionate about presenting the opportunity to join your fathers' group because you are confident that it will make a father's life better in several ways. You dress well, but you avoid gaudy or over-the-top clothing choices because you're aware that may turn people off. The Salesman wants people to know he's a success and is interested in helping people be a bigger success in their own lives. If this doesn't sound like you and you really want to be a group facilitator, you need to understand The Salesman's essential importance.

Sales, especially for people in the social service environment, is often associated with the ripe odor of rotting compost left too long on the kitchen counter. I don't do sales, you may protest; I'm a social worker, a parent educator, a group facilitator. Well, if you want to get good at running groups, now is the time to get over your squeamishness about sales and marketing. Your first job is to convince recruits that this program is a useful way to spend a number of their valuable evenings, and persuasiveness is a key element of sales and marketing.

Convincing potential group members will be easier once you own how important and powerful this experience will be for them. You need to awaken the memory in your own DNA that screams, "Groups save lives." In ancient times, the survival of a community depended on groups of men gathered around the fire. In our own chaotic, topsy-turvy world, the survival of our communities is still dependent on men of goodwill gathering in life affirming groups. Whether you are situated in urban communities with high rates of fatherless families and community violence or suburban communities with high rates of father absence and divorce, our culture needs to recreate space where men can go to heal and grow emotionally and relationally. Fathers' groups are an excellent venue to build healthy connections between men.

The Salesman archetype is one of the first you will need to manifest to run an excellent group. However, this archetype rarely leaps to the front of the list of roles that group leaders consider identifying with and implementing. Latent or not you will need to activate The Salesman. Very few dads sit around thinking, "Damn, what I really need is to sit with a small group of men and share my feelings." This instinct comes alive in men's groups, but it is not as strong as the sex instinct. Similarly, we are unlikely to encounter multimillion dollar budgets lined up to spend on ad campaigns that show how joining a men's group will help people feel as stress-free and satisfied as the taste of an ice-cold beer. You are charged with being the primary marketing firm for fathers' groups and just like the big ad agencies do, you need to understand human psychology and link your service to your potential customers' needs.

Benefits of Salesmanship

Fortunately, science and common sense are on your side so, unlike some major corporations, you won't have to claim toxic sludge is good for you in order to articulate the benefits of joining a fathers' group. You will need to embrace salesmanship.

Decades of research have documented the improvement of just about every positive outcome a parent could desire for his or her child when the father is involved in safe and responsible ways, including:

- increased academic achievement
- decreased acting out
- higher family income
- lower rates of teen pregnancy,
- lower rates of teen delinquency and the list goes on[3].

As families and societies, we desire the benefits that fathers' involvement provides. It's your lucky job as a fathers' group facilitator to have this plethora of benefits at your disposal when recruiting for your programs.

Obviously, though, it's not enough just to be able to detail your program's desirable benefits to a potential recruit. A fresh BMW 5 series sedan has a lot of benefits I would enjoy, but it's out of my price range. A good salesman identifies a qualified buyer by asking questions. Whether you recruit potential program participants at their children's school, over the phone with contact information given by a social service agency, or at a local barbershop, you let the recruit know about this great service you are offering and find

---

3 Vermont Legislative Research Service (April 3, 2012). Is there discrimination against fathers in child custody adjudication? Burlington, VT: University of Vermont. http://eclkc.ohs.acf.hhs.gov/hslc/tta-system/family/Family%20and%20Community%20Partnerships/new%20parental%20involvement/fatherhood/building_blocks1.pdf.

out if he is eligible to participate. This is sales work and your group benefits from you applying these skills.

In a way, you also benefit from not being a typical salesman. You have a program to "sell" whose long-term goal—improved father-child relationships—is worthwhile, as are the short-term outcomes such as increased academic achievement. And fortunately, the number of potential recruits is much higher than if you were selling luxury automobiles so you need not complain of having a small pool to draw from. Virtually every father or father figure could benefit from participating in a fathers' group. Even a Michael Jordan at the height of his game could tweak his skills a little, and possibly just as important, he could feel satisfaction from serving as a mentor for another player. One of your duties as The Salesman is to identify how the service you are offering satisfies a need in your recruit by asking him questions and listening to him. Then pitch your program as a scratch for his itch.

Finally, after providing basic facts, asking some questions, listening to responses, and pitching the benefits of your program as they could apply to your recruit, we arrive at one of the most important duties of The Salesman: you have to ask for the sale. Many of us are afraid to close the deal because we fear rejection. Get over yourself! You will be rejected more often then you are accepted. That is no reflection on you or the quality of your program. Some people reject something because they don't understand its value. Many people choose McDonald's over healthier food because they are focused on short-term gain rather than long-term benefits. That's their choice. However, you should not let people walk away or get off the phone without making them an offer to get to the next step by saying, for example:

"So, would you like to come check out the program?"

"Can I schedule a time to talk more about our group?"

"Can I call you back after you think about it a little more?"

You must be assertive in describing the benefits your group offers, linking those benefits to the needs you have discovered in your recruit and asking him to participate in the next step of the group process. No one else will do this for you—not the recruit, not your supervisor, not a website.

The Salesman is focused on the bottom line. He's interested in getting people in the door. He knows that once fathers arrive for their sessions, the other archetypes will make the group work. The Salesman realizes the necessity of asking the question that closes the deal and he's confident enough about the group's success to ask for recruits' participation. If the prospect says no, the Salesman expresses gratitude and moves on to the next potential member.

Sales is a numbers game. When you ask prospective members to participate most people (maybe as many as 90 percent) will say no. You just have to ask enough people to get the numbers you need to start a group from the 10 percent or so who will say yes. You may have to invite, recruit, or hand flyers to 100 people to get 12 to 15 men to join a group. That's okay; those 12 men will thank you so much for being persistent with them that after a while, your confidence will increase so much that you will do everything in your power to keep the next rounds of recruits from missing this great opportunity. That's salesmanship!

Facilitator Example

Several times I have had the opportunity to recruit for fathers' groups at child care centers that had over 100 children attending.

Very few of the children came in vans, which meant that 100 parents, other family members, or friends rushed through the doors within a 60- to 90-minute period to pick up kids at the end of the day. The bulk of adults arrived within the last 30 minutes of that window. I knew I needed to connect fast with as many people as possible to introduce my program and, more importantly, I needed to get a substantial number of contact numbers so I could follow up with prospects.

In this setting, speed and efficiency were vital. I couldn't afford to spend a lot of time with each person during the rush. The goal here was basic: get agreements that I could call at least 20 people each time I recruited at the space. Near the front door, I set up a table with flyers and a tri-fold display board like high school students use in science fairs. My board had photos of dads from previous groups interacting with their kids and some quotations from graduates saying what a great experience it was. A picture speaks 1,000 words so I was maximizing my presence.

As expected, most people passed by me initially saying they were too busy to speak, but many slowed down to look at the photos of dads with preschoolers and this was an opportunity to engage them in conversation. I told anyone who stopped that we were starting a similar program at this day care center in a few months and I invited them or their partner to join. I got a fair number of positive responses with this kind of recruitment. I also learned something unexpected: about a third of the parents picking up were men, but in focusing mainly on them I failed to speak with the women. In time I realized that a woman can be a great channel for communication with a man in a family, so after a few such recruitments no adult got ignored.

I also developed a quick way to approach the folks who were not slowing down to look at the photos. I handed them a flyer, looked them in the eye and said quickly and clearly, "Less arguments, more harmony." Who doesn't want that? I could see by many expressions that this jogged people out of their complacent dash to pick up kids long enough to wonder a bit about this program. On return trips a few of these parents were more willing to pause and talk to me about the flyer in their possession. Studies show that people don't change their behavior the first time they hear of a new product or service. It can take 10 or more exposures to a product for a new customer to become comfortable with the idea of changing their brand of juice or altering their regular weeknight routine to attend your group.

Participant Example

You're destined not to be the only salesman in the group. Everyone is selling something if only their worldview. Most of the men in your group are willing to give you the benefit of the doubt and not push back against the nurturing father perspective you are promoting. However, every once in a while you'll get a dad who wants to persuade the group away from a core value that your program promotes. Group members will have many differences of opinion that you don't need to confront directly. But if a natural salesman in the group tries to contradict your vision of the group, you will need to use one of the other archetypes (see The CEO, for example) to limit his advance.

Once a charismatic dad in my group was encouraging the other dads in the group to join him in doing a block watch type of activity to make the neighborhood safer. He was persuasive in his description of our group of community fathers patrolling the streets, recruiting other men and advocating for family-friendly neighborhoods. This was a great idea except he wanted it to happen during the time our group was meeting. That work was not on the agenda for our circle. I told him we were definitely continuing to meet on Tuesday evening as we had been. If he wanted to organize his community watch on another night and men from the group wanted to join him that would be great. I might even join them sometimes. He wasn't interested in making the extra effort to set up a whole new venture; he just wanted to usurp what I had created. Don't let that happen to you.

An even more common occurrence involves a dad who's trying to sell a worldview opposed to what you are promoting. This often comes up around physical discipline. A man will strongly advocate for corporal punishment and try to persuade other participants that your more nurturing parenting practices are not effective. This is a great opportunity for you to showcase your product. This guy's sales speech often ends with the famous, "My mom beat me and I turned out okay."

You need not go for the jugular here. Avoid the slam dunk comeback, "You turned out okay? You're unemployed, on probation, got three kids with three women who all hate you and you owe 20 grand in back child support!"

It's better facilitation to talk about the benefits of more nurturing parenting and how they generally give us alternatives to physical discipline. It's not realistic to expect participants to completely change their behavior in a few months, but as long as people are thinking about new ways of doing things and moving in a healthier direction, you should feel successful.

Another not uncommon occurrence is an honest to goodness salesman (in network marketing, automobiles, financial services, etc.) who gets wind of the small group you've pulled together and asks you for permission to present his agenda to the men you've recruited. Those folks' agendas are usually not in full alignment with what you are facilitating. So why would you give the fruit of your hard work to another salesman?

Shadow

By Shadow, I am referring to the unresolved, not yet enlightened aspects of an archetype. The Salesman has a big shadow. Many of our cultural impressions of The Salesman are negative. We see him as a money hungry, tackily dressed, say anything to make a sale lowlife. Many of us consider the sales profession beneath us when in reality, we all engage in sales of one type or another. Even if you are only selling your personality and skills to get a minimum wage job, that's still selling. What people don't like, and shouldn't support, is a salesman who will say or do anything to make a sale. You clearly do not want to be one of those.

It will be up to you to recognize when the Salesman Shadow makes his unenlightened, unresolved aspects evident in your work. Consider the focus we've placed here on recruitment. Even though you have a valuable service, it may not align with every recruit's needs at this point in his life. There have been a couple of times when I was recruiting for the program and I had tell the father I was talking to, who was willing to attend, that he just wasn't a good candidate at the moment. One guy was referred by a staff member at another agency and as we did his assessment interview, it sounded like he had been bouncing between being homeless and living in an abandoned building. He admitted to using crack "a few months ago" and had gotten clean with no treatment. His kids were in foster care and the mother of the children was AWOL. He clearly needed support, but he just wasn't ready for the fathers' group. Had I invited him in just to get the numbers I wanted to start, I would have regretted it. So I gave him the number for a substance abuse program, even though he seemed unwilling to check it out. Allowing people to join your group who are not ready is bad salesmanship. Your reputation and program will both suffer. Don't do it.

Fathers' groups are amazing for the right people, but not every dad will be in the right state to benefit at the time you meet him. Don't oversell.

Recommendations

1. Allow your enthusiasm for your program to affect your recruits. Be bold in proclaiming the benefits of your program. Practice being enthusiastic when you are alone and in front of the mirror. Save your shyness for the library. Know you have something valuable to offer the men you meet.

2. Understand the benefits of your program. Whether you are selling cell phones or fathers' groups, you must understand the competition. Who's your competition? The status quo methods of relationship malfunction and family disharmony. You are offering concrete methods to improve your recruits' lives. Use research statistics, stories from graduates in the groups, examples from your own life.

3. Listen to what your recruit is telling you about his own life. The best salesmen let customers sell themselves on the product. People have NEEDS. Your job is to match your prospect's needs to the service you are providing. In order to do that you have to listen to him and know your program. For most fathers this will be a great match for them. I have literally HUNDREDS of men who are grateful I came out of my shell and pumped up my program to them. You can do the same!

Power Question

When you believe in your product, it's easier to sell. Make a list of 5 to 10 answers to this question.

Why do you promote your groups enthusiastically?

2 The Scientist

Affirmation

I know what works in my groups.

Description

To some extent, I'm introducing the archetypes in order of their appearance during the course of forming and facilitating groups. But this is a non-linear journey so you will encounter plenty of exceptions to a sequential rule of thumb. The Scientist, though, is a fundamental attitude you will have to incorporate to facilitate groups. The Scientist is a straight up, no-nonsense character. He dresses neatly and soberly; you might imagine him wearing a white lab jacket and thick-lens eyeglasses. He's conservative by nature and on a mission. The Scientist has an idea or hypothesis, and he tests his hypothesis using exact steps that he or others may follow as he dispassionately records the observations. He doesn't need a flamboyant personality to carry out his role, he just needs his clipboard and his stopwatch and his determination—these will overpower any shyness he may have. The Scientist knows the group is a laboratory and he needs to make sure the required elements are present in the mixture.

The Scientist's love for statistics makes him valuable in group facilitation. Not only can you use your own recently gathered data about what works and what doesn't work in a group, The Scientist's expertise makes it possible to access data that other facilitators have recorded—resulting in patterns to learn from and include in proposals for funding and evaluations of performance. Of course, data gathering represents only a partial picture of what makes a group facilitator and The Scientist's role significant. Data need a shape to fix around, a design with goals and steps usually known as curriculum.

This brings up a common question about running fatherhood groups. What curriculum should you use? Some of The Scientists who preceded you have recorded their results in the form of series of activities that are sold (or in a few cases, given away usually because tax dollars have already paid for their creation), so that future group leaders do not have to recreate the wheel. You need to match the curriculum you use to the audience you target. Some curricula focus on young fathers, some curricula focus on incarcerated fathers; other curricula specialize in Black fathers or Christian fathers, and so on.

However, it's crucial to understand the curriculum is not as important as the facilitator. A great facilitator can make a lousy curriculum sing, but a lousy facilitator can ruin even the best curriculum. That being said, there are several good fatherhood curricula on the market. The one I used most often was The Nurturing Father's Program by Mark Perlman. If you compare various products you will see core similarities and other stylistic differences that may remind you of the car market. Automobiles all have similar parts because of their shared function. The type of vehicle you end up purchasing will have to do with your personal tastes, lifestyle and pockets. Once you have the car—or the fatherhood curriculum—the task of driving is basically the same.

If you think of the "science" of driving a car, there are certain key behaviors that govern turning, backing up, city driving, highway driving and other actions. There's also a creative side of driving, an artistic side, that I will cover in another chapter. But a driver, or a facilitator, must get the science of the behavior down first. And even though we may be using different "vehicles" (i.e., curricula), the driving techniques will remain similar.

Benefits of Time Management

The most important skill for The Scientist to acquire is timing. The full value of group interactions cannot be realized unless The Scientist manages the time required for each activity during each session. Before you walk into your group session, you must understand what the agenda is for the session and how long each activity will take. I know some of you artistic types are pooh-poohing this necessity. You believe in intuition and feeling. So do I; these tools have their place but you must have a structure that provides a basis for your intuition. Some of you will want to walk in and wing it and this will work sometimes. But you will be a much stronger facilitator if you have a preordained script that you can choose to flex away from rather than walking in and thinking it's all right to leave the whole game up to chance.

All decent curricula will give you a structure for how long each activity will take, and you should time that according to the hour you start your group. For example; if the curriculum has three activities that are designed to take 20, 40, and 30 minutes and your group starts at 6:00 pm, write your agenda like this:

6 pm – Activity 1
6:20 – Activity 2
7:00 – Activity 3
7:30 – End

I know this seems basic, but you don't want to find yourself adding up the minutes in your head while intense psychological interactions are happening all around you.

By using time based methods to organize group sessions, you make the necessity of paying attention to your group members easier to manage. However, a curriculum's activities aren't carved in stone. Allow yourself some flexibility with the timing, but don't move too far away from your schedule or you may miss important activities that come later on and you'll appear rushed. After working with a curriculum for several cycles of sessions, your sense of timing will get better; you may decide you want to skip one activity in favor of one you feel is stronger or more appropriate for your group's particular needs. Not all curriculum writers are geniuses and even if they were, sometimes you will have a better idea of how things run for the population you are working with because you are present with these fathers on an ongoing basis.

Since timing is one of the most important functions for The Scientist, you will need some tools for moving from one activity to the next and this is something you can customize for your sessions. It's good to give group members a heads-up on each activity's place within the week's agenda so they get a sense of when you will move on, and it's fine to encourage everyone to have responsibility for moving on to the next activity in the curriculum. Here's an example:

"I'm sorry, I'd love to keep going with this, but the curriculum says we have to move on now. I think you'll like the next activity even more, they build on each other."

Keeping a session moving along brings up the other most crucial function of The Scientist: You have to make sure everyone gets a voice. Forget about any images you might have of a scientist who stands in front of a class and gives lectures. That's a teacher. The Scientist is a practitioner. This archetype lays out the experiment, the exercises in each activity, and he allows the participants to experience them. While some participants use their memories of school as a frame of reference and start calling the group a class, I always discourage that term. A class has a more hierarchical nature than a group, which is more "flat" and open. This means that as you facilitate, you should not be on your soapbox railing at the guys during most of the session. Your job is to make sure everybody's voice gets heard.

It is The Scientist's job to equalize floor time. As we discuss group archetypes, you will notice some participants are prone to clown around (The Rascal), remain silent (The Recluse), or talk a lot (The Pastor). You will recognize these roles pretty quickly. You might already have noticed them during your initial assessment with the men; certainly by the time the participants attend their first group session with you, some participant personality types will become obvious. Of these types, The Rascal and The Pastor will use lots of group time if you let them. However, The Scientist knows from experience that he must hold everyone to task in order for the experiment to have every chance of success.

Facilitator Example

Since timing is such a crucial part of The Scientist's role, let's choose an example that demonstrates this element. In the first few minutes of a group session, it may be especially hard to transition from one of the other archetypes to The Scientist. You've been schmoozing with the guys, helping them relax and feel comfortable and—because you're super-attentive to the time—you know you have to start the session's first activity. This is literally like taking off one hat and putting on another. You use your body language and your voice.

With a quick look at your watch you say something like, "Okay, guys, it's five past now. Everybody's not here, but we want to let latecomers know that we get started as soon as 'critical mass' is here. There's so much good stuff to do tonight and the longer we wait, the more we are going to miss. So let's go around the group with the icebreaker."

All the facilitation roles are *leadership* roles. You are the leader of the group. The Salesman is dealing mostly with one-on-one situations in which he is promoting the benefits of membership. The Scientist is responsible for all the men in the circle as he gathers data on them and controls the time spent in group sessions. As facilitator, your overall role is that of leader. If you don't lead, the next strongest person will, and trust me, he will not take your group where you wanted it to go. You must embrace The Scientist side of your overall role:

- step up and start the group,
- move from activity to activity, and
- end on time.

If you don't, you are abdicating your responsibility and people will not follow you. They do not come out to sessions to hear an egotistical participant talk about himself all night. That may be interesting for a few minutes, but not for two and a half hours!

For the same reason, you have to move the conversation along from one person to another. That's your job! No one else is going to make sure shy Rafael gets his turn to talk about how his father used to take him down to Dudley Square to watch the men play chess. The Scientist is rational about equalizing time allotted for each member's input. He says things like:

> "It's five past and we're going to start even though everyone isn't here yet. That way, we'll have enough time for everybody to check in."
> and
> "Excuse me, Bob, that's been a little more than 3 minutes. We're going to have to move on now so everyone gets a chance to speak."

After awhile, you'll discover if Rafael doesn't share, the entire group is diminished. Group members' experiences have an impact on one another and you never know what comments or reflections will spark a revelation in another participant. So yes, Rafael, we really want to hear what you have to stay.

Participant Example

It's good to have other men with The Scientist persona in the group because they will help you keep track of time. If this is not your strength you can also assign a group member who is naturally more aligned with this archetype to help you keep track of time. Welcome his support. Deputize him to watch the clock for you. This will empower you because it shows you know how to delegate.

The Scientist participant will have other assets to offer the group. If you know he's used some of the new relationship skills between sessions and seen a positive outcome you could ask him to describe what changed. Obviously, just listening during the group is not enough to change a man's conduct at home. The Scientist participant may be an early adopter of the new parenting strategies you endorse, and allowing him time to speak about the shifts he sees in his life at home will inspire the other men. As long as you've laid a good foundation for your hypothesis, The Scientist participant will be a worthy assistant.

Shadow

Ah, the Mad Scientist, one of society's favorite stereotypes. The Mad Scientist appears when the rational mind is allowed to dominate emotional and intuitive intelligence to an extent that creates irrationality. He is so taken with his capabilities as a data gatherer and timekeeper that he is immersed in—"mad" about—facts and objectivity. To paraphrase Gandhi, the Mad Scientist has forgotten that the goals and the means to get there are the same thing. Problems arise with The Scientist archetype when you allow the need for order and logic to override feelings when you are interacting with people. You must keep things moving in the group, but you've also got to remain aware of the need for leadership that applies exceptions to the rules about time.

In reality, it's impossible to assign every participant the same two minutes for check-in or five minutes for responding to a particular exercise. If you follow any curriculum too closely you risk destroying the group. The curriculum does not run the group, the facilitator does. The map is not the terrain. If you do not demonstrate appropriate flexibility when allowing participants to speak or deciding when to move from one activity to another, the men in the group will begin to feel you are an unfeeling robot. They will not want to entrust you with their deepest emotions and memories. Scientists in society are often respected, but not always liked—unless they blend their predominant scientist qualities with other, warmer qualities.

The most important thing to remember about The Scientist shadow is to keep this set of traits in check by showing some of the more nurturing qualities we will talk about soon. The Scientist is essential to the delivery of a great group, but by himself he is too dry and unfeeling to generate the emotion necessary for skillful bonding. The Scientist can also seem aloof and objective, unable to really connect with the men in a meaningful way. By himself, he tends to be too cold to inspire the men in the group to open up and share about their lives. So, keep track of time and activities, but remember they are merely a means to a much greater end.

Recommendations

1. Plan the activities you intend to complete each session with a minute-by-minute agenda. Even if you decide to modify that agenda when you get in the group (which is reasonable and likely), you will have a baseline to work from.
2. Make sure all the participants, within reason, have an equal number of minutes to speak during each session. Keeping the energy circulating is crucial for group dynamics. Let people know this is your goal so they can help you stay on track.
3. Choose a curriculum that satisfies most of your requirements and become proficient in its use. Then begin to experiment with the activities to see how modifying the timing and content affects the moods and outcomes of your group. Incorporate your own ideas. Write your own curriculum!

Power Question

Spend ten minutes writing as many answers as possible to this question: Why are you confident that your fathers' group helps dads?

3 The Mystic

Affirmation

I see the Truth in my group.

Description

The Mystic is a different sort of archetype than what we've been dealing with so far. The Mystic is concerned with making the invisible visible or, at least, becoming aware of the influence of unseen things on that which is seen. The Mystic is an ancient archetype that is common across cultures. He prioritizes the spiritual world, but is not a religious figure per se. He operates outside the dictates of religious dogma by maintaining a strong connection to the heart and intuitive forces. He may be unorthodox in appearance and can arouse unease in people who are primarily focused on a conventional lifestyle.

The Mystic is important in facilitating fathers' groups. He is a respected elder figure (even if young in body, an "old soul" as they say) who can step outside the highly structured role that men are supposed to play in society. The Salesman and The Scientist, though different, are both more conventional than The Mystic. The Salesman and The Scientist often reinforce behavioral restrictions that discourage fathers from growing beyond preordained roles for men. These traditional roles have been changing as men take on more of the nurturing aspects of parenting that previously were reserved for women. The Mystic is a powerful archetype that supports men in growing beyond what we have been.

As in society at large, The Mystic remains somewhat hidden in a fathers' group. Unlike The Salesman and The Scientist, he is not there to play a highly visible role. His strength comes from a deep stillness inside the facilitator. He represents a contemplative element of the fast moving drama that occurs every session. As facilitator, you must act with enthusiasm to get men to come to your group, but after you get their attention you need to slow down at some point, listen and intuit the deeper places they are coming from. The Mystic reminds participants, as it says in the Bible, "Be still, and know that you are God" (from Psalm 46:10).

One of the most important roles of The Mystic in fathers' groups is the silent watcher who listens and reflects back the deeper meaning of what the men are saying. You must be active at times when you facilitate and, at times, you must be still. The Mystic represents the quiet, reflective energy that is present in all men, but undervalued in our cowboy loving culture. We like our leaders to be brash, assertive, action oriented. The value of stillness and listening has been lost, especially in "developed" parts of the world. Successful fathers' group leaders must model the value of listening deeply—with the heart—to the men in the group. When we do this, we hear on a deeper, more intuitive level. When fathers in your group experience the satisfaction of being listened to in this way they are more willing to try it at home with their families. Thus, we demonstrate how listening to their children and the mothers of their children can rescue families and relationships.

Benefits of Active Stillness

The Mystic's quiet, reflective energy benefit the facilitator and the group. This archetype understands the nature and value of reciprocity. Through your active stillness, you demonstrate that deeply intuitive part of yourself and share it with those in your inner circle of friends, brothers, cousins and others. The fathers' group is an inner circle of sorts. You nourish the men in the circle and you are nourished not only by your giving, but by what you receive in return. The reciprocal energy that flows when The Mystic is active is a wonderful dynamic to experience. You amaze the men in the group with your insight and the fathers in the group will convey remarkable insights that stem in part from having been listened to.

When this dynamic is under way, it is a powerful demonstration of The Mystic's capabilities. Wisdom comes from a space deep within you and sparks revelations around the circle. You seem to know more than you do because you have tapped into the "group mind". Similar to a collective unconscious, the group mind is a place that holds the truth and secrets of all the men in your group. Your awareness of this place comes with responsibility for the effects that the group mind can spark in a fathers' development. This responsibility, for The Mystic, is a humbling experience. When you are applying this archetype as a facilitator, you set aside your ego—the human tendency to elevate status and authority.

By discarding your ego miracles happen, an immeasurable benefit of The Mystic. Seeing and accepting fathers as they are, you help them see and accept themselves as they are—a powerful place from which to change.

The benefits occur alongside challenging moments. Often your stillness reflects unacknowledged pain in a man. For example, a father appears angry while sharing a story of abandonment or betrayal by a loved one, either parent or partner. It feels comfortable and powerful for him to feel anger. I rage, therefore I am. The Mystic does not meet fire with fire. He absorbs it and reflects it back as truth:

"You must have been sad," he says.

Or, "It sounds like you were hurt."

Sadness. Hurt. Emotional Pain. When you offer statements such as these, you are not acknowledging traditionally masculine feelings. Instead, you are acknowledging truth and your truthfulness strikes a chord. The resonance is felt around the room. Of course, he was sad. Of course, he was hurt, everyone thinks. But they remember, that's not what he expressed. He said, "I was angry."

And because everyone in the group empathized with the man's anger, they wonder if sadness and hurt compels their own rage. They naturally reflect on their wounds, and the wounds they have inflicted on children, partners and others.

The Mystic's presence in these moments distinguishes him from other archetypes. The Salesman and The Scientist don't breed these types of revelation. They move too fast and they have other intentions in mind. The Mystic's deeper awareness is drawn from stillness and silence and receptivity. Society has prejudged these attributes, but these are not really feminine qualities. They are *human* qualities that we were taught to associate with women. To be compassionate human beings and parents, men must learn to demonstrate these qualities as well.

Facilitator Example

It was the first session in a 13-week fathers' group. The men were sharing about their family of origin. This was hard for many of the dads. Most of their fathers had been absent for most of their childhood, or abusive to them and their mothers. However, it felt good to talk about it and be listened to by a group of other men.

When it was Charlie's turn, he said, "My mother and father were both drug addicts. From what I heard, my father was never around and my mother put me up for adoption at five years, I mean days, five days old. My foster mother took me in and she raised me in a good Christian home. I understand that my real Father is in heaven and is always looking out for me so everything turned out okay."

It was a studied response. It felt like he was used to saying those words. It also felt unreal.

The Mystic said, "Wow, Charlie, I get that your foster mother was really committed to you and introduced you to a Christian life and I'm happy for that. However, I just want to go back to your bio parents for a minute."

His expression shifted, almost imperceptibly.

"You said, you 'were adopted at five days old?'"

"That's right."

"That must have been really hard for you as you were growing up."

"No, my adopted mother was an angel and she gave me everything I needed."

"Hmm. You must have felt abandoned by your birth parents."

"Yes, I did." Charlie didn't make it past those three words before he started to cry—hard. Thirty-five years of blocked emotion started being released in the circle of men that had been strangers until an hour or two before.

Unlike The Salesman and The Scientist, there is no strict curriculum device that will tell you when to say "Hmm." You have to feel it. If you are afraid of feeling your feelings, you will be uncomfortable being present when someone else feels his and you will miss these moments. By slowing down and remaining aware of what's happening inside you, you open the door to awareness of what's going on inside the men in your circle. That is The Mystic.

By the way, Charlie looked ten years younger after he'd cried, and all the other dads in the group looked at him with a newfound love and respect.

Participant Example

The Mystic is, by nature, an elusive archetype. When a participant really nails it, his presence can be a great blessing in the group. More often I've seen participants display shadow qualities of The Mystic which we will discuss next. It's more common for group participants to embody external religious qualities which align more with The Pastor archetype which we will discuss shortly. The Mystic is harder to notice in participants as he tends to be more internally and experientially focused. However, one brother I remember channeled strong aspects of The Mystic.

He was a tall man, deep into ancient Egyptian culture and had studied several mystery traditions within the African Diaspora. He was knowledgeable about the Kemetic tradition, Five Percent philosophy, Gnostic Christianity and the Sufi in Islam. Even his dress distinguished him from the other men in the group: he often wore a fez (a type of hat), and he also wore an ankh or some other symbol that indicated he was seeking something not confined to the material world. I mention this because his presence alone had an influence on the group. The impression we got about him wasn't just due to his height or his regalia; he possessed a calmness and insight that deepened our conversations about family and relationship.

Maybe one of the reasons The Mystic archetype is not very common in participants is that the business of operating a family tends to draw a man away from his mystical inclinations. Kids, house, job, wife, commuting, a hectic lifestyle and inundations from the media all tend to draw a person away from that still, quiet voice within that is so dear to The Mystic. The spiritually inclined may find the louder, charismatic voice of The Pastor more comforting to their station in life. This Participant Mystic, let's call him Blessed because he did have an unconventional name as well, was the single father of a teenage son and had somehow managed to keep massaging his inner compass while raising a son on his own.

Like a true Mystic, he was not one of the most talkative men in the group, but the other fathers showed respect when he spoke. He words carried weight. Other dads often sought his wisdom one-to-one during our dinner break or after the circle ended. Blessed seemed to enjoy this role of quiet mentor to other group members and to be honest, I think this is one of the reasons he signed up. He acknowledged throughout the group sessions that he was growing as a father and a man from doing the exercises, but when I first described the structure of the program to him, I believe he saw it as a place he could teach the brothers in his understated way as well. Neither of us was disappointed.

This brings to mind The Salesman archetype. Sometimes recruits, who seem very advanced in a discipline such as mysticism, finance, or physical health, will state explicitly or seem to imply that there is nothing they could learn from joining your group. Acknowledge their success in whatever field they are concentrated in; but unless they are involved with emotional skill-building groups with other men, you can guarantee they will gain new knowledge and skills in a well run fathers' group. Promise them that; let them know their base of knowledge will be demonstrated in the group sharing segments, and share your expectation that you and the other fathers will benefit from them.

Shadow

When I started this chapter, I just wanted to jump ahead to this section because The Mystic has a strong shadow that often seems more popular than the actual archetype. The Mystic Shadow tends toward spacey pronouncements such as, "Spirit tells me you are angry at your father." Avoid channeling disembodied spirits during your group sessions. Spiritualism is popular with segments of the population, but like other religious pronouncements this is better left to a community based on beliefs around that practice. Again, when we talk about external elements of religion in The Pastor chapter, we'll talk about how to use that archetype in culturally sensitive ways. The same caveats hold true for the more internally focused interests of The Mystic.

It may be even easier to fall into the Shadow when using The Mystic archetype than others because to begin with, the territory of The Mystic is largely based on intuition, feelings and unseen forces. The Mystic asks you to think about and proclaim what you know to be Truth. In reality, you will not always have definite answers to give participants, nor should you, people will own the answers they discover more than answers they are given. Sessions may proceed in a direction for which your curriculum offers little to guide you.

Sometime you will have to guess a bit. Sometimes your intuition will be bull's eye correct and sometimes you will be off.

It's important to remember: you could be wrong when you dig deep inside people's situations, looking for the Truth. If you find no collaborating evidence when you proclaim your Truth to the group, you may have missed the point. You may even have misled group members. Problems arise when you insist you have the Truth—especially about other people's lives—and other people do not see it your way. That's called demagoguery and it's a trait associated with narcissistic dictators, not successful group leaders. Be courageous enough to share your Truth and humble enough to let it go if you find no resonance in the external world.

Recommendations

1. Make some time outside of every group to quietly reflect on the various personalities in the group as individuals and as a collective. Be open to flashes of insight about people or situations.

2. You don't need to share every insight you have with group members as a whole, or even individually. Sometimes your intuition can simply help you guide the group and the participants in a certain direction that you may not have been aware of before.

3. If you have a powerful insight before or during the group and have an urge to share it, do so. It may be important for the father to hear the perspective you want to share with him. If it resonates, don't get too excited and start to herald your ESP-like powers. Be humble; you got lucky. Similarly, if your Truth is not widely reflected in the group, don't try to beat participants over the head with it. Let it go; maybe it will make sense later, or maybe it won't, but you did your best. Over time, your intuition and hunches will get stronger and more accurate.

Power Question

Ask yourself this question when you are experiencing conflict in your group. Remain open to seeing the deeper truth that you may have missed:

What is the Truth I see in this situation?

4 The Mother Hen

Affirmation

I take care of my own.

Description

For those who thought all the archetypes that influence a men's group would be masculine—surprise! Each person contains masculine and feminine qualities. A well run fathers' group awakens qualities in men, like compassion, nurturance and intuition that are generally associated with the feminine. This is a good thing. A well run group exposes the lie that men do not embody these qualities and that women cannot be assertive, independent and logical—qualities generally associated with men. Before I describe specifically how The Mother Hen archetype benefits your group, we need to address gender stereotypes briefly.

To be a master group facilitator, you need flexibility to demonstrate attitudes and behaviors that go beyond what society traditionally has considered masculine or feminine. Let me be clear and strong on this point. Being nontraditional does not feminize men. It humanizes us. Compassion and nurturance are not the provenance of women alone. Logic and assertiveness are not the domain of men alone. The notion that men are better than women and the qualities that are more closely associated with men are more valuable is nonsense. Men and women are complementary and sometimes competitive, but our intrinsic worth is equal because we are all created by and connected to the same Source. How we display that connection in the world varies from person to person. Some qualities, however, are clustered around specific cultural groups.

At a deep level, becoming a nurturing father challenges the poison of patriarchy. Patriarchy is the erroneous idea, widely accepted in our world, that men are intrinsically more valuable than women. The practice of patriarchy is based largely on physical strength. The threat of violence works well to keep oppressed groups in check. The greater upper body strength of most men has gone a long way to defining the types of interpersonal relationships men and women engage in.

Violence and the threat of violence have played a critical role in intimate and social interactions between the genders. Hence, protection of the family (including adult females) has been one of the key roles for fathers across the globe. When a father—or group of fathers—cannot protect the members of their family, their value is diminished and they become marginalized. That's the main reason why rates of fatherlessness in the U.S. are highest in the black community. The African-American experience began with men losing all power to protect their families at the same time that women experienced continuous violence and threats of violence to themselves and children. Four hundred years later, we are still trying to recover.

While the ability to protect and provide is still demanded of fathers today, the job description was expanded by the impact of the Women's Movement. When the mostly middle-class white feminist vanguard underwent an epiphany in the 1960s and '70s, the resulting shift changed the social norms of what was expected of all women and men, including fathers of every cultural group. Hordes of men didn't just decide overnight they wanted to be at the births of their children. Mothers decided they wanted a more natural birth experience and that, naturally, included fathers. A critical mass of men didn't suddenly decide we wanted to change diapers and feed babies in the middle of the night. As more mothers started working outside the home, they demanded that fathers help out more with child care.

But something magical happened when fathers started taking on more of what had been women's parenting roles. We discovered what women had been getting giddy about all these centuries. Babies are amazing. The indescribably fresh smell of a newborn, the profoundly deep stare of an infant, the absolutely sincerity of a preschooler, these acts and others spoke of miracles far beyond what many of us found in Sunday morning sermons. By spending time with our children, that most important quality of unconditional love was fostered in many men in a way that work or church alone could not touch.

In addition, by understanding the birth process better we gained a better understanding of other kinds of strength. In my own case, before our first child was born, I intellectually believed my wife was my equal. However, growing up in a patriarchal culture, there was a part of me that didn't really believe that. I imagine that's how white people of goodwill have to struggle against the false idea of racial superiority. But I tell you, when I saw my wife squeeze a human being out of her body, a whole new level of appreciation for woman's worth was also born. This deep appreciation of motherhood—of womanhood—paves the way for our deep practice of fatherhood—manhood. That baby doesn't get in there by himself!

When we move into that deep space of manhood, we are less anxious about, really unable to, deny the qualities in ourselves that are traditionally considered feminine. Aspects of yin and yang, or anima and animus as Carl Jung called them, are in all of us. Because women have been so undervalued by so many of the world's cultures, the gender dynamic is out of balance. In some countries, female infanticide is considered a viable option given the high cost of dowry and low prospect of female income. In more enlightened places, some fathers are still disappointed when a daughter is born—especially if it is the first child—but being more "sophisticated" we pretend not to mind. The basis of this disappointment is not just that men prefer boys. Fathers know the kind of shit a woman has to go through in the world and we fear for our daughters—because we know how we are.

Benefits of Flexible Roles

In his 2002 book *How Can I Get Through to You? Closing the Intimacy Gap Between Men and Women,* Terry Real quotes a Masai warrior elder whom Real has asked what makes a good warrior. The African elder tells the middle-aged American, "I refuse to tell you what makes a good *morani* (warrior), but I will tell you what makes a great *morani.* To know what it takes to be fierce and what it takes to be tender and to know when to be each."

There will be times in a group when fierceness is required, but as a group facilitator, you need to make sure you initially influence and hold your charges with the tenderness of The Mother Hen. Years ago, a male friend shared a relationship framework with me that struck a chord. He said, "Relationships are a journey. A man's job is to set the destination and get the couple there. A woman's job is to make the journey comfortable along the way." We can temper the rigid gender roles perpetuated in this idea by recognizing the value in each role and the flexibility that can exist for either gender to play either role. But, in a fathers' group, it is the facilitator's job to play *both* roles. So you not only have to get the men there, you have to make sure it's comfortable along the way. This is the role and the benefit of The Mother Hen.

Set up a nurturing learning environment. Arrange the chairs in a circle so the sense of hierarchy is diminished. Participants will still look to you as leader in this configuration, but they will get the best experience when everyone is seen, heard and valued, and a circle is the best structure for that. For optimal effect, remove all the tables and other impediments from inside the circle. Anything in the physical environment that separates the participants is discouraged.

The open circle facilitates conversation, allows men to see one another easily, and helps The Mystic read the group's subtle energy. There is less opportunity to hide. People still find ways, though. Their best defenses, clothes, language and expressions remain intact. There are a myriad number of ways for a participant to feel safe by setting up boundaries using one of those three devices. Vulnerability is key to the powerful, non-sexual intimacy that develops in fathers' groups. The ability to cover up their thoughts and feelings to some degree is what helps reluctant or resistant participants feel comfortable enough to even attend the group and gradually increase their openness. The circle is also a direct contrast to the most common learning environment participants have been exposed to: a teacher standing in front of many rows of desks and chairs, lecturing to students. One teacher in front of a class allows students to easily hide and ignore each other. This presentation model discourages sharing. Boredom soon follows.

When men walk in the first night and see the circle of chairs, they are put on alert. A circle tells people: You will be asked to contribute. We want to hear from you. Because most people were socialized in the top-down, teacher-knows-everything, you-know-nothing model, an open circle can be terrifying, definitely uncomfortable. Many people seek ways to resist this kind of feeling and it's up to the facilitator to ease their minds. As The Mother Hen you imbue the circle with safety—your body language, speech and expressions emphasize the answers each participant seeks are within. Through conversation with peers and gentle guidance from a peer leader, each father discovers what they need to know. They can take ownership of their feelings about parenting and feelings about life.

To successfully run a group you need not have a degree, but you must be well integrated. You must have learned how to regulate your emotions, how to breathe properly, how to listen reflectively, how to share your own feelings with aplomb. You can learn those things without earning a master's degree in counseling (or a related discipline), but you have to work on yourself. The Mother Hen is supportive in this pursuit. She is flexible and accommodates different learning styles.

In addition to emotional nurturance, physical sustenance is another important Mother Hen-related duty for your group. You should try hard to provide some sort of meal for the participants. No matter what the economic level of the community where the group has sessions, people will be drawn in when you offer a meal. Observe that even well-heeled professionals are more receptive to attend a meeting if food will be available. Men who are stretched economically will be even more motivated to attend your group for a meal.

Breaking bread together has always been a good icebreaker that can help reduce people's resistance to the open circle. You can experiment with having food at the beginning, middle, or end of the program. Each time slot has its pros and cons. One pro to having food in the beginning is that people are more likely to arrive on time; a con is that the session will then have to go a longer amount of time without a substantial break. Having food in the middle of the session breaks up the group's schedule nicely, but when you have mid-session meals, there are some jokers who always seem to arrive right before the food is served. While this is still better than them not coming at all, feel free to use the other group members to encourage everyone including tardy members to come on time. Use The Scientist's emphasis on time management so that The Mother Hen can provide the benefits of sustenance.

Facilitator Example

Like a Mother Hen rounding up her chicks lest they wander off and stumble into danger, a master facilitator will round up his participants before each group. As The Salesman you've got to convince fathers to attend and get their commitment. As The Mother Hen, you've got to call them to remind and re-inspire them, at least before the first few sessions until they catch the excitement internally. You may even have to pick some of them up. Most of the participants should be able to get to sessions on their own, but I make the offer to transport some guys if that makes the difference between them attending or not. If your budget allows and you've got a decent public transportation system in your location, giving transit passes or stipends can help also. The nice thing about picking up men before and dropping them off after is you get a chance to bond and learn things from them on the way.

One brother named John was a member of a group I facilitated and fortunately, he lived near my office and home, which were close to each other. So we got into a routine: the two of us rode together to the program each week, a 20-minute drive. In addition to the bonding time during the drive, other benefits emerged. John got to help with the set-up of the room and I could depend on him being in the circle to help break the ice when the other dads arrived. On the way home, his presence was even more beneficial because he helped me debrief from the session.

Each group session generates a lot of energy, and you'll have vignettes and incidents from the evening playing in your head when you leave. Even though the "official" co-facilitators and I debriefed about the group before we left the program site (including any follow-up we needed to do before next week), riding home with John allowed me to reflect more slowly on interactions during the group and get a participant's perspective on how things went. As we got to know each other better John felt comfortable sharing concerns he had about other men in the group which sometimes confirmed feelings I was having and sometimes reminded me that John was struggling to overcome a lot of limited thinking on his own part. Even though we discussed incidents that happened in the group which involved other participants I was careful to maintain an ethical boundary about any personal information I knew about other men from my role as facilitator.

Participant Example

Participants in the group can also manifest The Mother Hen attitude toward their peers. Near the end of one 13-week series I was leading, after we had all gotten to know each other pretty well, one of the men broke down at the end of a session as he talked about money problems he was having. He was living in a shelter unit with his three children and receiving financial assistance from the state. It wasn't enough to hold everything together, though. As we started to close up for the evening his armor dropped, his voice got choked up and he began describing how he didn't have any money to buy food for the kids that week.

It was a moment of real intimacy in the group. Even though it meant we would go over a couple of minutes, which I never like to do, I let him express himself, and in doing so, model vulnerability for the other men. I was about to say, "Let's talk after the group to see what we can do." There may have been additional concrete social supports that we could have hooked him up with. Nor was I above reaching in my pocket for some dollars to help him through the week. Before I could get that out, though, one of the other men in the group said, "I'll loan you some money! Let's go to the ATM when we leave here."

The group members all started to applaud, the brother in need looked like he had seen an angel, and The Mother Hen participant looked like he knew it is blessed to give (or, at least, loan). This was not the moment for me to offer an alternative plan, although I did stay abreast of the loan to make sure The Mother Hen Participant got repaid for his generosity.

Shadow

The participant story above cautions what may be the most dangerous element of The Mother Hen's Shadow: doing more than what you are able to do as you try to take care of someone else. We frequently hear about birth mothers who feel overwhelmed because they are constantly doing for other family members without taking care of themselves. And it's almost cliché to hear about those in the social service arena who are burnt out from trying to help others without first ensuring that their own physical, mental and spiritual health is in order. That is the shadow side of The Mother Hen: not establishing healthy boundaries.

Although the incident above refers to a participant Mother Hen, it could have easily been about a facilitator who reached into his pocket and gave *what he could not afford*. In fact, that was the outcome of the loan described above: the good Samaritan did not listen to the brother's problem with deep enough awareness. He didn't need someone to cover his entire debt for that week, but that's what the Mother Hen offered to do. As I listened along with the others that day, I had a bad feeling about it, but not enough to step in and apply boundaries to their financial interaction. A few weeks later, I got put in the middle when the receiver did not pay back what he had promised by the agreed upon date. Because I had seen it go down in my group and didn't stop it, I bought the bad debt, ate some of it and the borrower was good for the rest.

Whether it's giving money or time (for instance, working unpaid overtime to drive a participant and his family to appointments), a master facilitator must learn where the proper boundary is for working with each member of the group. We need to empathize, reach out and go the extra mile. But when you've gone many extra miles and still no end is in sight, you must learn how to balance your involvement with the group so you don't damage other relationships in your life, including that most important relationship with your own personal integrity.

Recommendations

1. Nurturing the participants is an important part of the group experience. Make the atmosphere conducive to open conversation by placing chairs in a big circle with no obstacles in the middle which promotes bonding and connections. If possible, include a meal or snack that nourishes the body as the uplifting conversation nourishes the soul.

2. Contact participants in between sessions to see how they are doing. Call the next day if a father had an especially emotional time with one of the exercises. Offer rides or other transportation to the program as much as your budget can afford.

3. Maintain healthy boundaries with the participants so you don't feel burnt out from doing too much to try and "save" the men who come to your group.

Power Question

Caring about participants and showing them you care in a way that they appreciate are two different matters. Ask yourself:

How do I show that I care?

5 The CEO

Affirmation

I use my power for the good of the men in my group.

Description

We've arrived at a favorite archetype of most men. Who among us hasn't dreamed of being the boss? The CEO is a powerful archetype that both men and women find attractive. Some might shy away from the role anticipating great responsibility and preferring to stay cloaked in anonymity, but not you. If you've gotten this far in your career the ambition to lead is strong in you, so let's unfold this commanding presence that can make you a better facilitator.

Ultimately, The CEO is charged with maintaining the smooth functioning and profitability of the group. However, control of a well run group is subtle, not overbearing. A police state is not therapeutic. If you come off as too controlling, even if people do return week after week, learning is compromised because the environment is too authoritarian. In this context, leadership involves understated confidence rather than the insecurity that forms the basis of much dictatorial rule.

While many people mistakenly associate a boss with overbearing command, The CEO does not define himself in arrogant terms. This archetype understands and values the group's development. A dictator's style threatens the all-important opportunities to take risks and be creative. Although many of us were educated in this manner, the dominant/submissive paradigm doesn't promote self-reflection and self-discipline. Participants who enjoy a heavily controlled environment (and there are many) may feel comfortable stifling their creativity and freedom of expression, but the goal of a well run group is to encourage each participant to become The CEO of his own company, i.e., himself.

Benefits of Management

Communication and connection are the products in a fathers' group, so the CEO's job is to make sure the stage remains free for the give and take of information. This requires that three conditions are met:

1) No person, including you, dominates the conversation.
2) No person, even the quietest, is consistently left out.
3) The conversation is conducted with respect and compassion.

Human nature makes these conditions difficult to manage. There's always someone who wants to dominate the conversation, someone who wants to hide from conversation, and someone who wants to rag on others.

Managing these conditions goes most effectively when you are aware of your own nature. If you have a controlling personality, for example, you need to balance it with other archetypes. For instance, the CEO is not the ideal recruiter. His persona is too directing for persuasion. The Salesman is a better choice to feature when you are encouraging dads to attend your program. However, you invoke The CEO when you are sitting with a group of men and several want to speak at the same time, while others want to hide in their chairs. As The CEO, you need to manage the dynamics. Fear of exercising authority causes unsuccessful facilitators to avoid this primary responsibility and their group suffers. But before you demonstrate The CEO's power, make sure you have already bonded a bit with your participants, using other archetypes, so people will accept your direction more graciously.

In order for you and the group to gain maximum benefit from The CEO's management, you need to identify rules for the group in the first session. Then when you need to refer back to the rules, it's not like you're the bad guy. Those are just the rules.

Speaking of rules, The CEO also has a role to play in time management of the group. The Scientist knows when transitions need to be executed; The CEO makes sure they are executed. An early opportunity to lay down the law involves starting and ending times. You must start as close to your scheduled time as possible. I know some of our people have a serious handicap in this area, but you cannot be one of them. If 6:00 pm is your start time, as the facilitator you need to be there by at least 5:30 to set up the location (or assist co-facilitators), check on details about the meal, make sure all curriculum materials are in place, and greet people.

As The CEO, you are the role model. You demonstrate the type of participation you want in the group. Great leaders create great followers because they were once great followers themselves. Fathers' groups develop as sacred space if you perform well. The CEO must be integrated in his own self-mastery enough that he can run the group without making it all about him. Tinhorn dictators are all too common in the CEO position. Small-minded, petty individuals who shouldn't be running an ice cream stand end up leading countries, companies, and fathers' groups. The effective CEO stimulates a well run group by demonstrating the benefits of managing himself first and the group participants only after that.

There are almost no benefits to gain from dominating the conversation without letting other men share the airwaves. This is a sure sign that your CEO is off track. Not valuing others' opinions because you know best is another indicator that your CEO persona is in danger. Not honoring the rules you have set up for the group is a big warning: you are misusing your power. The end result of a narcissistic CEO is that the participants will not have as positive and life enhancing an experience as they could. Work on yourself to avoid these costly errors.

So if the program starts at 6:00 pm, you don't want people to show up at 6. Actually, you want them there early so you can START at 6. Ask people to arrive at 5:45, because you know many people will get there later than you ask and you want the group to be ready to start at 6. And while you cannot start with none of your participants present, as soon as you get critical mass, anywhere from one-third to one-half of your participants present: Begin!

Basically, you want everyone to know this is a timely program and you respect their time commitment. Don't keep them past the scheduled end time even if you start late. Skip some of the activities rather than going over time. Do not give in to the temptation to keep people later than you promised. Even if the conversation is going magically—and often it will be, you can see light bulbs going on over people's heads left and right—still you need to show you are in charge of the time. Do so graciously: give people a few minutes' warning before you wind down, then End On Time. Even if everyone is excited about the extraordinary dialogue taking place, close the circle at the designated time.

No matter how excited people feel in the moment, on reflection, they will feel cheated if you go longer than you said. Most of the participants have something important to do after group and if you keep them late one week, the next week they will think, he kept us late last week. It was a good talk, but I've got to put the kids to bed after the group (or update my Facebook status). That's more important than a great conversation with the guys.

If people want to stay and hang out awhile after the group, provide a space for that to happen for about 10-15 minutes to allow the energy to calm down. But unless someone is in crisis, use these minutes to start your post-session clean-up. After all, you've got important stuff to do after the group, too (if you don't, find something important to do after group). This will allow The CEO to have his down time which is important to his overall health and will prevent The Mother Hen's Shadow from emerging. If someone is in crisis, take enough time to come up with a short-term plan for the night and follow up with them the next day. Remember: It's late, facilitating a group is emotionally exhausting, and you need to model good self-care for the participants. Take care of yourself!

Another, even more complex role for The CEO is traffic cop, regulating communication. Early in the group, I tell participants I'm the traffic cop; when the fathers get excited as they invariably will and start talking over one another, I decide who gets to talk based on as objective criteria as possible. Whoever I heard speak first, or saw their hand up first gets to speak first. If one of the more quiet group members wants to speak, but one of the more loquacious brothers keep beating him to the floor, I may go with the guy who hasn't had so much air time to even things up a bit. But right or wrong, it's my prerogative to decide and there are no reviews of the play. The call on the field stands.

It's important to divide up the speaking time as evenly as possible. If you get the last word on everything or allow yourself to give monologues on every topic, you will, at best, bore the participants. At worst, people will stop coming. And definitely you will lose much of the power and wisdom of the group. You are far less interesting than the group as a whole and The CEO recognizes this benefit and seeks to maintain it.

This brings up a truth about group dynamics. The importance of the group is greater than the importance of any one individual in the group—including, nay, especially the group facilitator. There will be some group members who want to talk constantly. There will be other group members who express neediness in their silence. Deal with their need for your own and the other group members' attention in a balanced way during the group (and in a balanced way in your available time outside the group, if necessary).

No one is served if you allow the group to be a stage for any one man's problems. The other men, being human, will empathize with the brother's plight, but will quickly lose interest in the group if it becomes more about one personality—including yours—rather than the unique group personality that develops. The CEO must guard against this with vigilance!

Another important function for the CEO involves divisive, unhealthy alliances. Although this is a parent education support group, in some ways it resembles a middle school classroom. There will be cliques, showboating and passive-aggressive behavior among participants. A common example is folks talking among themselves. It's often about something sparked in the group that seems too personal to share. It could also be seditious remarks about other people in the group, including you.

If two people become overly invested in each other in ways that disrupt the group, usually speaking to them during a group session will resolve the issue. Verbally highlight their conversation, since everyone is aware of it anyhow, and ask if there's something they want to share. If not, ask them to stop talking so everyone can hear from the person who has the floor. That way it's not about you. It's about the group and especially the person who is speaking. Asking a couple of times and maybe even joking about splitting them up usually works. If they persist, tell them during the next break you will have to split them up. Then don't hesitate to do it. In my experience, most people stop with just a warning.

Facilitator Example

The CEO is the ultimate manager and sometimes, okay, oftentimes, he needs to serve as the group's police officer. I actually tell participants that I will be the traffic cop when we have conversations. It's my job to enforce the rules we have identified. The main rule I emphasize is that we speak respectfully in the group, including no cross talk, no cussing each other out, etc.

I remember facilitating a group at a correctional facility and needing to manifest The CEO quickly. We were sitting in a circle with about one dozen men who had been locked up at least five to ten years and were now in a pre-release setting. These men had the typical range of charges you could expect in long-term inmates and they were all fathers.

The guards brought all the men into the room we were using and did one check-in during the 90 minutes we met, but otherwise it was me and a phone on the wall if things got out of control. I did several 13-week series in that setting and the emotional dynamics in the group were similar to what I experienced in community programs. However, one time, two of the fathers got in a disagreement about some aspect of parenting—I don't even remember what, let's just say it was physical discipline of kids since that has strong proponents on both sides. The outcome was that these two inmates started back and forth comments that got pretty passionate.

The two disagreeing men were pretty equal in size. They were sitting opposite each other; they each came in at over six feet, north of two hundred pounds and they looked like they spent much of their time in the weight room. Compared to them, I was small at 5'8" and a buck forty. But I had the authority, and these two were not going to snatch it from me in my group. As soon as I realized they had stopped listening to my traffic cop instructions on who had the right to speak, I dramatically jumped into the middle of the circle and stood directly between the two of them. This was a preemptive strike, neither of them had even risen from their chairs.

I had the entire group's attention. I said, "Whoa. I'm facilitating this group."

The two men stopped talking and I shut down that conversation with the rap about how we all have to listen to one another, we have to remember the rules and whose job it is to enforce them. The men simply let the disagreement go after that.

A few other times, other groups' conversations have gotten so heated that I have used the jump in the middle of the circle maneuver. That example was particularly memorable because of the location and the size of the dads involved.

Participant Example

I don't encourage participants to adopt the role of a CEO participant. Certainly it's important for them to be CEO in their own lives and to help out during group sessions. But, having multiple participants feel like they need to manage the group will lead to chaos. When you are working with a co-facilitator, you should share the duties of leading the group in a pre-arranged manner with that person. Your leadership should be subtle and even handed, allowing the participants to fully experience the group activities without feeling responsibility the flow of events.

the

Shadow

Considering how useful The CEO can be, in one sense it's surprising he's gotten a bad rap. But The CEO's less than stellar reputation is built on that old truism, "power corrupts." In governance, business and even the family tree the CEO has come to represent male ego run amuck. Images of kings feasting with a court full of sycophants while villagers starved; corporate takeovers where executives fire competent workers and double the load on others to increase shareholders' profit; fathers yelling (or worse) at their wife and kids, and then locking themselves in their man-cave; all these represent the Shadow aspect of The CEO.

If you let the Shadow elements of the CEO rule while facilitating a fathers' group, you are likely to cut off people while they are talking because you have a clever point that you just have to make at that moment. You may find yourself giving directives to dads about what they should do in a given situation rather than helping a dad figure out for himself what is the best thing for him to do. Or you find more and more of the presentation time taken up with exciting stories of your wonderful family and life.

Because self-evaluation is challenging, a co-facilitator can be helpful to bring you back from the brink of ego gratification by checking in with pre-arranged codes to tell you he thinks you are talking too much. Also, make sure you have time after the group to debrief with your co-facilitator (see the archetype *The Lover* for more wisdom about the co-facilitator's dance). If you are working alone, you have to maintain that guidance for yourself. If you take the time to get grounded before the group and afterward reflect by yourself (see *The Recluse*) or with a colleague about how things went, you should be able to notice when you are being overly controlling and can correct yourself immediately.

If you are unsure whether you're exhibiting overbearing, ego-centered CEO behavior, try talking to an experienced facilitator about it. You tend not to get honest answers from asking people in the group or from written evaluations. People often don't want to hurt your feelings. It's easier for them to just stop coming to the group. And most people have not been in a powerful, well run small group. Participants are used to family and workplace dysfunction, so they may not be capable of describing for you what is wrong with your group. But they will feel it in their gut.

Recommendations

1. Exercise group rules and norms to maintain a strong container that's able to hold the passionate, potentially volatile mix of thoughts and emotions that develop.
2. Running a group is a heady experience. Keep your ego in check by reflecting deeply when alone and checking in with someone you trust.
3. Don't take yourself too seriously. Recognize that you and the participants in your group will make mistakes as part of the learning experience. Embrace them and learn!

Power Question

Maintaining a servant's attitude in this position is not always easy, but it is essential to running a successful group. It demands that we ask ourselves:

How do I use my power to serve group participants?

6 The Pastor

Affirmation

I speak Truth with love and enthusiasm.

Description

The Pastor is an interpreter of sacred mysteries. Unlike the Mystic who inwardly discerns the Truth and shares it subtly, the Pastor studies the Truth in outward form and speaks it loudly.

This is an important archetype because he makes visible the faith-based elements of facilitating fathers' groups. According to the Pew Forum, about 90% of U.S. citizens identify with a religious tradition, including 78% who associate with a Christian denomination[4]. Consequently, most men in your group will identify with some religious tradition. This is good to know because religious practices can be an enormous motivation for people to adopt healthier and reject more toxic behaviors. The Pastor can provide instrumental guidance along these lines.

Still, a description of this archetype must include some of the reasons why facilitators fail to embrace The Pastor in group ses-

---

4 Pew Forum on Religion & Public Life (2012). Report 2: Religious beliefs & practices/social & political views. Washington, DC: Pew Research Center. http://religions.pewforum.org/reports.

sions. Even though facilitators may appreciate the leverage of pastoral motivation to encourage changes in behavior we must also remain aware of the challenges and risks involved. The Pastor is responsible for presenting his moral beliefs in an environment that may not be congruent with his ideas. For The Pastor to be an effective facilitator archetype he's got to accept some diversity of beliefs, and some pastors have a hard time with that.

You want to be honest with the group about your own beliefs. You should have strong views about your faith and, as a successful facilitator; you need to accept other people will have strong views about theirs as well. Unlike "polite" society, a good facilitator doesn't avoid talking about something as significant as faith in order to push divergent views under the rug. These can be some of the most interesting conversations. The Pastor facilitator maintains integrity having these conversations when he makes sure there is no undue influence on participants to join any particular religious organization.

With this archetype it would be good to even broaden your definition of church and consider that a well run fathers' group has many of the same characteristics of a spiritual fellowship. First, there's a group of people gathered for a high ideal, a collective purpose. There's a catechism, an organized set of questions posed for the purpose of acquiring knowledge and absorbing appropriate ways to learn and change. There's a facilitator and most of all there are transcendent moments. Almost every week, one or more interactions occur that lift awareness beyond the ordinary confines of daily life. When you facilitate these heart-opening conversations about family and faith, you have stepped into the role of The Pastor.

Benefits of Heart-Opening Conversations

Many practitioners in the field of social services miss a golden opportunity to use their clients' religious sentiments to leverage changes in behavior. This occurs because the practitioner doesn't know how to talk about religion or spirituality without proselytizing, attempting to convert others to his religious beliefs. Most victims of proselytizing find it distasteful. Not only is it unethical in secular human service programs (because of the unbalance of power between professional and participant), it's also illegal if your program receives government funding (because laws require that we uphold the separation of church and state). That's fine because I'll show you how you can get all the benefits of leveraging a participant's religion without resorting to proselytizing.

If you operate out of a faith-based organization which receives no funding that prohibits proselytizing, go right ahead and sell any gospel you believe in. That's your right as a believer. You may lose some participants who have strongly held but differing religious views from yours, but you need to be true to your calling and you may please those with views that align with yours.

Although faith-based fathers' groups are popular, most of the groups I work with prohibit proselytizing. And unless you prioritize gaining converts for your religious organization over the particular needs of the men in your group, I encourage you to refrain from conversion-based activity within your fathers' group. There may be times when your religious understanding totally aligns with a member of your group and he naturally seeks you out for faith-based counseling anchored in your specific religious tradition. Build with that brother in a venue that's outside your fathers' program.

This is important because it can be damaging to fathers and families for a man from another religious belief system to come to your group and be told overtly or subtly that he needs to convert to the facilitator's religion in order to be a good dad. There are enough religious wars already happening on the planet. Fatherhood and family really can bring different groups of men and women together in love. Christians, Muslims, Jews, Buddhists, Hindus, Pagans and atheists all love their children. We can use fathers' groups as a vehicle to develop cross-cultural understanding, but only if we see and know our truth while we accept others' understanding of truth as well. This is essential to using the Pastor archetype wisely. It's not just your attitude that's of concern here. If an individual father or group of believers from a particular religion is in your group, you need to make sure they do not intimidate people from other faiths from speaking about their truth.

This is not as hard as it sounds and it may not come up frequently, but you should be ready to deal with it. The Pastor needs to be clear on this because if he avoids this issue, he loses one of the most powerful motivations for individual fathers in your groups to grow and change. Since The Pastor seeks to speak truth and thereby motivate people, you should make a sincere effort to gain an understanding of each group member's religious, spiritual or faith beliefs and incorporate them in your group dialogue. The importance of these beliefs to the person who holds them is huge and as you work toward greater and greater intimacy in your group, it would be neglectful to leave God out of the equation.

The Pastor reminds participants that moral and personal development are the keynotes of a well lived life. A few years ago I came across a poster of an African dad in his mid-30s and his son who looked about 5. The father was helping the son walk across some large rocks at the edge of a river. A caption above the idyllic scene read, "Fatherhood, the most important job you'll ever have." Immediately the image annoyed me and I couldn't hang the poster in my office until I made one alteration. With a marker I changed the message to read, "Fatherhood, one of the most important jobs you'll ever have."

Although I was prepared to passionately defend my action, none of the hundreds of fathers and professionals who passed through my office acknowledged or complained about my revision. To me, it is clear that being the best child of God—spiritual aspirant (whether Christian, Muslim, Jew, Hindu or other)—is the most important job I will ever have. I believe that atheists can be great fathers, too. I believe, for all parents, our most important job is being the most evolved, loving human being possible. Fatherhood is a great role in which to practice that skill. Being a good parent aligns neatly with that mission, but it does not transcend it. If you put all or all of your best eggs in the parenting basket when it's time for the children to go on their adult path it may be harder to let them go than is necessary. Don't lose yourself in the journey.

If you recognize all along that parenting is only a part of your own spiritual quest, you will never let your kids down by making them more important than God or Truth or Love. Helping all the parents that come to your group uncover this truth is another role for The Pastor as he is the one who reminds group participants of the highest spiritual laws. When you practice the role of The Pastor, group members get to experience how deeply and greatly you believe in Truth and Love.

Facilitator Example

I had my first face-to-face with Derrick during the opening session of a Tuesday night group. My goal is to do an individual intake with each participant before the program starts. Sometimes scheduling prevents this and men come to the group after only speaking to me on the phone. Such was the case with Derrick, a 30-year-old man from Barbados who was the single father to a seven-year-old boy. Derrick wore a frown when he showed up and complained about having to take time out of his busy evening because the Department of Children and Families wanted him to become a better father. His son went to an adjacent room to enjoy age-appropriate activities with our on-site child care team and Derrick joined us in the circle.

One of the activities that evening was to visualize being with your father when you were a boy—imagine how he looked and all the ways he interacted with you and your mother. Many men have no conscious recollection of their dad. If that is the case, as it was with Derrick, we ask them to explore how it felt as a young boy not to have a relationship with their father.

Some men try to imagine their mother instead of their father using the old line that their mother was their mother and their father. Derrick went to the "I never knew my dad; my mother was my mother and father" place and in response, I remarked that I after hearing that line scores of times I began to push back against the idea.

Respectfully I suggested, "Your mother could be super-mother, but she could not be your father."

To men like Derrick who maintained this idea, I pointed out the ways moms and dads are different—not the least of which is they are two separate people, of different genders, with different histories that have to learn to co-parent a child.

But one of the most powerful arguments against this idea of mothers as fathers is what I told Derrick: "If you believe your own mother could be both your mother and father, then by extension it must be true that the mother of your child can be both mother and father to your baby. So, basically as a father you're saying, 'I am not necessary to my child.' And I know that is wrong."

Derrick went beyond the place he was at when he arrived that day. He said for the first time, he was able to acknowledge a deep pain over the loss of his father. The stony-faced urban warrior broke down and cried as he felt the tremendous hurt of missing his dad throughout his childhood. The other men in the circle heard him and their faces softened as they watched the man they had just met walk swiftly out of the room with a burden many of them knew all too well. I left my co-facilitator in charge of the group and went out and stood with Derrick. Initially, I just stood with him quietly supporting his deep expression.

After a few minutes, he spoke: "I'm sorry. I didn't mean to cry."
"Don't apologize," I said. "It was good to finally let some of that out."

That was a transcendent, cathartic, healing moment. It was like being in church. People go to church to find something bigger than themselves—something they can believe in, something that inspires them to lead a better life and to fellowship with other people looking for the same thing. When Derrick broke through that wall of defenses around his dad's absence, he healed some of his pain and gave himself a better chance to be emotionally available for his own son.

As facilitator, you create a space that connects a man to his higher self and aligns his awareness with a deeper purpose in his own life. The original counselors were pastoral counselors and as a facilitator, you are with your group members partly to offer guidance, encouragement and many of the other dimensions we typically associate with counseling. And that makes you manifest The Pastor.

Participant Example

A lot of Pastors will join your group. It's a common personality type for men who are willing to participate in a fathers' group. The group comes together in love and the most common experience most men have of a fellowship in love is church. Plus, the group gives a voice to the often unacknowledged reality in the public sphere of how powerful church, spirituality and church leadership is in people's minds. And finally, because The Pastor is at root a helpful figure and participants will be anxious to lend a hand where they see the possibility.

In one group I facilitated there was a young Muslim brother who enjoyed sharing an encouraging spiritual perspective with his peers. In this case, the archetype might be called The Imam. He often quoted verses and ideas from the Koran to emphasize the direction he was trying to head in his own life and to make suggestions when other men were feeling confused. This brings up the fine line between conversation and evangelizing. I did remind him on a few occasions that not everyone shared his worldview. He accepted this as a tolerant man of abiding faith will, with a tacit understanding that of course, people have free will to go off track. But he seemed personally obligated to share his understanding of truth with us.

The pleasant, and maybe even ironic, element of his procla-
mations was that even from a secular point of view the advice he
offered was reasonable. It reminded me how much of "religion"
aligns with common sense. Avoid excessive use of intoxicants, he
told his fellow participants, stay away from other men's partners;
be honest with your own partner and kids. He had been raised in
a Christian church, but broke away from the faith as a teen and
ran the streets as a drug dealer, user and womanizer. Eventually, he
found his way out of self-destructive and community destructive
behavior by becoming a Muslim. He had the simple faith that if
it worked for him in his degraded state, it would work for anyone.

Many of the elements of his faith taken piecemeal provided
inspiring guidance for other men in the group. As facilitator, I
allowed and encouraged the piecemeal advocacy. However, whenever he strayed into language that sounded like he (and his faith)
had the only way to truth, it was my job, as facilitator, to make sure
he did not become a religious demagogue in the group.

Shadow

The above example had the potential to stray deep into the Shadow
of The Pastor: religious demagoguery.

In contrast to The Mystic who helps each participant connect
with his own intuitive truth, The Pastor helps participants align
with established religious laws and mores. Rather than relying on
people's sense of what is the right thing to do, The Pastor encourages people to know the truth from study of scripture. Acquiring
knowledge in this manner tends to make one more dogmatic in
its execution and this is where the Shadow emerges. The Pastor is
a bit of a hard-ass. He has a tendency to be a little full of himself,
which ironically interrupts the flow of divine spirit through him.

If you catch yourself believing you have the only way to be a great facilitator or father, you should remember there is more than one way to be successful.

The Pastor speaks with an authority that goes beyond what most archetypes bring. His enthusiasm for faith-based study results in supreme confidence in his position and he may not acknowledge potential blind spots easily, if at all. This faith can overcome many obstacles; however, if The Pastor doesn't know when to back off, he can become obnoxious. It's also hard for him to laugh at himself or his position. The Pastor is at risk of taking himself too seriously. It's also easy for The Pastor to get confused about how powerful and wonderful he is. If The Pastor forgets where his juice comes from he might lose his humility and ironically some of his spiritual power along with it.

Recommendations

1. Be willing to talk about your own religious or spiritual beliefs in a way that honors whatever faith walk others, including atheists, are on.
2. Help participants align their parenting actions with the highest principles of their own faith tradition. Leverage their beliefs to support the parenting principles in your program and vice versa.

Power Question

The Pastor has great authority in interpreting Theological ideas for his group. In doing so, it is important to avoid shaming participants. Answer this question:

How do you tell the Truth with Love?

7 The Lover

Affirmation

I connect with love.

Description

It is important to have a co-facilitator work with you when you start facilitating groups. Hence, you can see one of the best ways to get in this game is by assisting someone who's experienced in facilitating fathers' groups. Eventually, you may be able to handle all the roles by yourself, but in the meantime don't ego trip; get help. It is possible to deliver a well run fathers' group with you operating solo as a facilitator, but it's easier and more fun to learn the ropes with a partner. Plus, by going alone, you perpetuate the Lone Ranger model of masculinity which fathers' groups inherently dismantle. Find a co-facilitator!

Even if you don't identify and train and coordinate with a co-facilitator, one of the group participants may naturally start to fill some of the tasks in this role so be open to a participant who could grow into a facilitator. It's not uncommon.

I've developed many great friendships from co-facilitating with other men and that's a fantastic outcome! A special bond of love and intimacy naturally develops with people you do this intense, emotional work with. Being guys, an underlying discomfort can exist around that. So let's put the gay question on the table right now. Some people might consider it remarkable that we got this far in a book encouraging men to be more emotional, vulnerable, and intimate without addressing homosexuality yet. However, this discussion is breaking ground a bit because in most of the fatherhood circles I've been in, men do not usually openly deal with same-sex relationships.

Although mores are changing, most men in the groups I facilitate, myself included, grew up in cultures where homosexuality is less valued than heterosexuality, to put it mildly. Often man-on-man sex is thought of as vile and disgusting. Woman-on-woman sex, while maybe not encouraged in this paradigm, is given much greater latitude. A problem with understanding and advocating for male intimacy as distinct from male homosexuality is, as men, we've learned to conflate love and lust. So when you bring a group of men together for the purpose of emotional bonding and generating love, queer (in both senses of the word) feelings and fears may become heightened.

Any meaningful exploration of The Lover as facilitator must include several facets: our tendency to confuse love with lust; our misunderstanding of The Lover role; the importance of this archetype for group facilitation, and our prejudice surrounding how men handle and mishandle love.

Benefits of Co-Facilitators

The Lover has the responsibility of creating a deep emotional bond among group members. This includes overcoming the fear of male intimacy. There's an unspoken idea in male culture that feeling love and affection for other men might suddenly lead to an all male orgy. Hence, we'll go a long way to prove how macho we are. After all, most of the time men feel love and affection, it's a prelude to having sex (with a woman). If we feel love and affection for another man what could that lead to? Most modern males' bonding rituals—watching or playing sports together, drinking and socializing, or playing video games—avoid deeper levels of emotional connection. In a fathers' group we learn to open the heart without activating the genitals. Men are used to competing with other men, either physically or mentally, so creating a male space that has a cooperative ethic allows men to grow in love and harmony with other men in ways that can feel unfamiliar, but ultimately very enjoyable.

Thankfully, this is also where you discover the benefits of bonding with a co-facilitator. In addition to the potential for acquiring a friendship and a professional ally, there are more practical, less charged aspects of working with a co-facilitator. Running a successful group involves a lot of tasks. You need to: contact and assess people, call and remind them before each session, prepare the session agenda and flip chart, greet participants when they come into the space, buy the meal and utensils, facilitate lively discussions, make sure everyone gets heard, begin and end on time, put your personal biases away and listen to participants, contact group members you sensed were traumatized by issues raised in the group, understand and suggest effective methods of parenting, and much more! That's a lot for one person to do.

It's far better for you and a co-facilitator to divide up the tasks. The division of tasks should be based on interest and compensation. The lead facilitator will need to do most of the planning and the work if he is getting most of the money. That's something to discuss and agree upon before the preparations begin. It's best to make a plan early and be flexible with implementation. For example, one of the most important roles of a facilitator is to keep the conversation flowing (and other more subtle forms of energy, i.e., unspoken thoughts). When two facilitators are managing the atmosphere of the group, it's a good idea to designate one as the play-by-play man and one as the color commentator. In televised sports, the play-by-play man describes the minute-to-minute action, illustrating with words what you are seeing. The color man explains the background and offers a context for what you are watching. In a group, the play-by-play man keeps the group sessions tightly aligned with the agenda, encapsulating and emphasizing important points that participant speakers make. The color commentator launches into related stories and visions and fables related to the action in the group. Sometimes the play-by-play man will have to bring back the color commentator as well.

Both roles need to be executed for the benefit of group bonding and growth. While it's possible for one experienced person to do both well, it's easier when starting out to divide these roles between two people. If one person acts in both roles, he must be very self-aware of his own motivation to speak as well as be able to read the group's energy as he is speaking.

Another benefit of working with a co-facilitator is that the intimacy and intensity required in the roles of co-facilitators provide great grist for the development of relationship skills. You have to be able to communicate on a deep level or you will get frustrated. Sometimes you'll get frustrated even when you do communicate on a deep level, because there is a disagreement in points of view. Human beings can be irritating when thrown in close contact with one another. My meditation teacher says her residential school is like a gem tumbler. She puts the rough stones in (her students) and by the constant friction of being figuratively tumbled against each other, rough edges are smoothed out and the stones come out shiny and beautiful. Marriage and family can serve the same purpose.

The fathers' group shares a similar experience. You will be figuratively rubbing up against your co-facilitator more than anyone else. But as the two of you start to shine together, a subconscious understanding arises between you. Some people experience it as telepathy. You begin to *feel* where he is going with his comments. When other participants in the group see and feel this synchronicity, they want to replicate that sort of relationship because it is appealing. The Lover is in the house! Co-facilitators working together can show group members the outcomes of love more clearly than one facilitator working on his own.

Men are accused of not having friendships as deep and long lasting as women. The idea of the strong individualist not needing others seems stronger in men more than women. But the radical act of two men, in a non-sexual relationship, sharing a deep emotional and spiritual intimacy is so attractive other men want to experience it because they sense the healing nature of the relationship. This need for male friends is obvious with young boys, but somewhere along the way many men lose it. That loss negatively impacts our ability to bond with our children and the mother of their children. The Lover's facilitation helps to reverse this inhuman trend toward isolation and fear of intimacy.

An element of friendship involves accountability. There will be times when you and/or your co-facilitator make mistakes. We may find it difficult to hold people accountable and love them at the same time. We all want to be loved and want people to think well of us. Sometimes our fear of losing the connection with a friend will prevent us from pointing out in loving ways that he messed up. We may let things slide until we explode or act out in a passive-aggressive manner. This may happen more in our intimate male-female hetero relationships than in our male-male friendships because we feel there is less at stake with our brethren. But as we start to explore deeper levels of male intimacy the stakes become greater and similar dynamics may develop. We may have developed a tendency to either let a problem go without addressing it, or to be an asshole about addressing it. If your model for confrontation is that popular male archetype, the drill sergeant—you get up in somebody's face because as the facilitator, you are the superior, dammit!

What's required, instead, is a more compassionate accountability that downplays our ego in the equation. As The Lover, you do not confront your co-facilitator in a hostile manner because you are their superior (even if you are their supervisor in this or other settings). Instead, you confront him with respect and empathy because you are role modeling nurturing. We must confront because we can't let the participants down with shoddy programming. Facilitators who come in late, don't prepare, constantly curse and repeatedly speak about others disrespectfully are not competent to run a program. If you are working with a facilitator who demonstrates some or all of these problems, you are going to have to talk with him. It may not be easy, but those behaviors will kill your program.

What this work demands is the more sophisticated response of staying conscious and working out difficulties. These communication tools are part of a comprehensive curriculum. You learn to struggle through the differences with your co-facilitator and as a result you each become stronger for not stuffing your reactions to a healing opportunity/crisis.

The connection that you share with your co-facilitator is beneficial for the health of the group and for the health of each of you as well. Male friendship is undervalued in our world. The stereotype of the strong, silent, loner man is harzardous to our connectedness and well-being. I went from being a young man with a few good male get high buddies to putting all my eggs in the marriage basket. My wife is still my best friend and I always *knew* other guys, but not until I started participating in fathers' groups did the healing power of male friendships become evident to me. Maybe you've obtained some of that through team sports-based relationships or fraternities, but coming together around the idea of healing relationships adds an extra onus to the intimacy that develops in the groups.

In a fathers' group, we come together to expressly learn how to connect in deeper ways with our children, which naturally leads to a deeper connection with our children's mother(s) and naturally leads to a profound connection with the men we are taking this journey with. I'll grant there is an element of "misery loves company" in some of this bonding:

"No kidding, your (child/girlfriend/wife) does that, too? I thought I was the only one."

But the more important element is that we strengthen our connections with other people. There is a long tradition of men sitting around the fire at the end of the day telling stories about our lives. Before I started doing fathers' groups, I mostly experienced that with other guys when we were getting high, but smoking eventually led to so many problems that I stopped doing it. I didn't realize how essential it was for my soul that I participate in a small group with other men. And while group facilitators gain bonding from the elements of working together and helping one another, all the men in a well run fathers' group become The Lover to some extent.

The Lover is a being who shares a love connection. We may recognize in experiences like these that we are not only soul mates with one person, but with all people. When we attain this level of understanding, whether we do so as facilitator, co-facilitator, or group member, we experience the greatest benefit of manifesting The Lover. It is so important, on so many levels, for men to acknowledge the love we feel without being creeped out about sexual orientation. Even for hetero guys, this practice of showing love with other men helps us relate to our sexual partners on more sophisticated levels.

What does it mean for men to share a love connection in a fathers' group? It means you listen to another man's story with respect and see elements of yourself in him. It means you understand a brother who becomes vulnerable and shares how his heart was broken in one of an infinite number of possible ways. It means you trust your friends in the group and the very power of the group container to hold your vulnerability so you *can* share how your heart was broken. It means you rejoice at the success of one of your comrades in a personal or professional sphere. It means, in short, you behave as a reflection of divinity, a true human being rather than a malevolent force that moves through the community sowing seeds of apathy, at best, or degrees of evil, at worst.

This may sound simple, but you know it's not easy. Our world, and especially the oppressed, violent communities that many of us come from, seems designed to bring out the worst rather than the best in people. I was running groups when 9/11 occurred and talk of tan men in terrorist cells dominated national conversations. As I met with several groups of fathers during that time, I reminded them that our group represented a nurturing cell. We were gathered not to take life, but to give it. The life giving spark in humans must be nurtured or it will be snuffed out. Our fathers' groups are a uniquely masculine place to practice brotherly love.

Just as you will vibe with certain co-facilitators more than others, some of the participants will develop special friendships with other men in the group. Some fathers share an affinity for creating music or playing sports or have kids the same age and they develop a friendship that extends beyond the group. This is beautiful, of course, and you need to make sure friendships like these don't create an unhealthy clique during group sessions. You and your co-facilitator will speak more openly about group members' behavior and character when you debrief and plan outside the group. Participants who meet outside the group will take the same opportunity to talk about other group members, except they may not be as compassionate to the foibles of their peers as you are. It's your job to make sure they don't come to sessions and start dismissing or making fun of more socially awkward or cognitively challenged members of the group, as can happen when cliques form. This is not hard if you nip it in the bud. If you let it get out of control, you could have a middle school class on your hands.

One of the unique features of a fathers' group run by fathers is that no women are present. This is important because men are typically used to women being more emotional and focused on relationships than we are. In fathers' groups we acknowledge a whole palette of emotions that most men don't access very easily or very well. Anger is, by far, the most socially acceptable emotion for men and the activities in your group should help dads get in touch with sadness, fear, jealousy, joy, and even excitement (about things other than sports and sex). But even though women are not physically present, their psychic energy plays a major role in group dynamics.

Not surprisingly, women are a major topic of conversation for men in fathers' groups. I am continually impressed with the level of discourse and insight that men demonstrate in a well run group. Yes, during each series I've run, there are one or two vocal participants who sport a misogynist bent. But I've discovered that most participants are open to exploring when they may be taking undue advantage of male privilege (even if they didn't call it that) and when a woman is being truly unreasonable. As a good facilitator, you want to lead people away from the blame game and focus on personal responsibility. Sometimes we just chalk things up to the mystery of women. Feelings don't have to be logical; that's why they're feelings.

Facilitator Example

The Lover is evident in almost every interaction between a facilitator and his group participants so it's hard to break out just one example. But here's a simple, yet powerful case in point. By midpoint in this 13-session group we all knew one of the fathers in particular was having a hard time with the mother of his children. José had a son with a woman who had an older daughter by another man and for four years José had been raising both of them like they were his own.

More and more in the group he started telling us things like, "I think I might have to step away from the situation until my son gets older. I just can't get along with this woman and it's gonna get ugly if I stay."

The other men in the group and I offered support and encouragement for him to hang in there for his son. We talked about strategies he could try that might help the situation improve, but he felt like he was already doing all he could and that her lack of ambition and combativeness were the primary causes of the problem. So I did what I often do with brothers who are going through a hard time and can't seem to find a resolution within the group space. I offered to meet with him individually. One bright Thursday morning found us in a beautiful urban park that was plopped right in the middle of our community. We walked and talked as some late morning joggers sweated their way around the perimeter of the park. Most of our early conversation was filling in details of our life before kids, stuff we had alluded to in the group, but hadn't been able to go into detail about because of time constraints.

Eventually we made it around to José's current situation with the mother of his children. I was disappointed that he felt like the entire relationship – not just the sexual/romantic part – with his son's mother was unsalvageable, but I respected his feelings. Soon after this, he did decide to limit his time with his son. He paid child support, but no longer sought visiting time because of the ongoing conflict with the mom. This hurt him deeply. Despite not seeing his son for weeks, José continued to come to the group. He got support from being with other dads, but it was hard for him to see the other fathers with their kids and hear the joys and struggles of being with them.

The Lover as facilitator became obvious to me when we celebrated the completion of the group about six weeks after José and I took that walk. During our last activity with just the fathers present, José shared with the group how much it meant to go for that walk.

He said, "Haji, I want to thank you for making time for that walk that day. It meant a lot to me and helped me sort out a lot of my feelings. As men, we don't always feel we can be open with other dudes cause they'll see us as weak or punks. But not only in the group, but by taking time outside the group, you showed you really cared and that meant a lot when I was going through that hard time – which isn't over, but at least I got more coping skills by coming to this group."

I was touched. And that's how you feel when you're The Lover facilitator.

Participant Example

Lots of guys want to be ballers or rappers. Most of us give up on those dreams by the mid or late 20s. For many of us though the dream lies just below the surface and only needs a slight inspiration to bring help it break through to the light of day. That's how it was with James, Willy and Peter. The three men were all in their mid-20s and had one or two children under five. They didn't know each other before they joined the dads' group, but they quickly discovered a shared love of hip-hop and desire to make and record rhymes. They still hoped to be stars.

At first these The Lover participants just excitedly talked about music and recording equipment during the break and after the group. But after a couple of weeks each of them started arriving before the group and sharing stories and rhymes before our group check-in. It was only a matter of time before they got together outside the group. Willy lived in a central location and had some kind of home recording equipment set up and by Week 4 they were the best of friends. I enjoyed seeing their friendship grow and only in my most paranoid, selfish moments did I fear their friendship might fall apart before the group graduated and one or all three of them might drop out of the program.

That didn't happen. Pretty much the opposite did in fact. They brought some background beats and the three of them performed a fatherhood rhyme together at the graduation. I haven't seen them on the cover of XXL magazine yet, but embracing The Lover participant added value to their own lives and to our group.

Shadow

One of the reasons that some spiritual aspirants renounce their families and become monks or nuns is so they can look on the entire human race as their family. If one is attached to one spouse and a couple of children, obviously you tend to put them above other people. To a lesser degree that is the danger of facilitating a fathers' group from The Lover archetype. Like other areas of your life, there will some members of the fathers' group with whom you feel a deeper natural affinity than with others. As facilitator it is important that you keep your sense of perspective with those participants and don't favor them over other men in the group. An obvious, or even subtle, favoring can lead you to overlook times when they may need to be on the hot seat, or you may subjectively align with them as opposed to other participants even when objective evidence may weigh on the other side. Learning how to love all the men in your group equally is great practice for equanimity in other relationships in our life, such as children, siblings, colleagues, etc.

Recommendations

1. Be open to feeling and expressing love with the men in your group. Meditate on what it means to love someone, to be Love when with someone. Of course, there is the physical aspect heralded in sexual relationships, but go beyond that. Ponder what it means to be in love. How can you show others that you love them? How can you be love?

2. Spread your love in the group as equally as possible. There will be those for whom you feel a natural affinity who will be easier to love. However, showing favorites as facilitator is detrimental to the overall health of the group. Try returning love for that which is unlike love. Experiment with forgiveness and acceptance in the group and outside of it. Forgiveness is a practice that helps love stay fresh and ever new.

Power Question

Talk is cheap, as the saying goes. Many men have been condemned for using the famous three words, "I love you," when the object of our affection was not feeling it. Thus, The Lover asks this core question:

How do you show your love?

8 The Warrior

Affirmation

I protect my group.

Description

You may be surprised at the inclusion of a martial archetype in a guide to promoting loving relationships. Yet, like the other archetypes, The Warrior symbolizes an energy that is required for successful groups. The Warrior represents both protection and advancement. In order for powerful transformations to occur in the participants they must feel safe in the circle and it is primarily The Warrior who defends the integrity of the group. Ignorant people, both in the circle and outside, will attempt to destroy what you have created. Don't let them.

The Warrior is a seasoned martial artist. Ever hear a good karate instructor talk about using the skills you develop in a dojo? He repeatedly tells his students, "Avoid fights. Don't use your skills frivolously. Most of the time you can safely and wisely walk away from potential violence or violation; however, if you have to fight, put your all into it and defeat your enemy decisively." The type of conflict I am talking about here is mental, emotional and spiritual. If a conflict in your group ever becomes physical, it's gotten really out of hand. Likely, you have dropped the ball on managing conflict in one of the first three realms mentioned.

The men you've inspired to come to the group, who've heard your call, who've experienced the intuition and structure and love of a fathers' group want more out of their lives. They want to realize the vision of more harmonious and intimate relationships you've described. They want to move beyond the limitations of fatherhood as it was defined for them and accept a larger role in the family than their own fathers held. It's a heady experience to have new vistas open up when you believed the horizon was narrowly, foolishly circumscribed. Some participants will want to move forward fast, others will want to linger in the status quo and a few will try to sabotage their own and other group members' progress into this brave new world of family relationships.

As leader of the group, you must exercise The Warrior at times, or those mired in the status quo or the realm of sabotage might divert you from your mission. The clarity of your vision is vital. The Warrior understands the terrain with the support of the other archetypes. It is through them that The Warrior knows what path to take. So, the first awareness necessary for The Warrior is to decide where you are going while understanding the rules of engagement.

The Warrior is charged with enforcing the rules of the group, spoken and unspoken. He works very closely with The CEO archetype. As an analogy, in a modern corporation, sometimes The CEO will make the decision to fire a person and when the terminated employee is informed, security—The Warrior—shows up to escort the former employee out of the building. In a smaller company, the

CEO may have to put on his Warrior hat to walk the employee out. As facilitator, you will be both CEO and Warrior.

Similar visions and directions exist in all the good fathering programs on the market. They all capture the zeitgeist of early 21st century cooperative parenting on our evolving planet. Ideas spread quickly across the interconnected Earth. As junk food emporiums proliferate internationally, so can good ideas. Fathers groups spread good ideas like the benefits of dads being empathic with family members; how to support equitable division of labor in the home and strategies for fathering without violence. In the current generation, men in Western countries have been dramatically more involved in child rearing than in times past and research shows that fathers, mothers and children have benefitted from that shift.

It's no coincidence that these life enhancing developments follow on the tail of significant struggles for freedom by oppressed groups all over the world in the late 20th century, such as Africans, Indians, women, and gays. As women sought a different relationship with men and money outside the home, men began to have a different relationship with women and children inside the home. This has been a great thing. One of the great sorrows of modern manhood is that many of us lost contact with the diverse spectrum of powerful archetypes that control our inner world. Rather, we have tended to embrace only the most hyper-masculine archetypes such as The Emperor and The Warrior.

However, The Warrior must defend and serve the circle while maintaining a high degree of awareness. Other aspects of our inner world will be described before this journey is over, but for now it's crucial to acknowledge that even The Salesman, The Scientist, The Mystic, The Mother Hen, The CEO, The Pastor and The Lover (and the other archetypes to come) play a necessary role in influencing the actions of The Warrior. Too often men are rewarded for riding roughshod over the more sensitive, intuitive elements of our consciousness:

"It's my way or the highway."
"Get up and walk it off."
"He who dies with the most toys wins."
"You gotta beat his ass."

We are told in so many ways to "Just be strong and go!" Without incorporating the other archetypes, it's easy to confuse these toxic messages with The Warrior affirmation, "I protect my group."

The Warrior's job in a fathers' group is to put down attacks against the modern model of fathering and help keep order in the group – using wisdom and compassion. Participants might say it's stupid for men to take over women's work in the family. Or a dad might say it's always been like this and God ordained that men don't devote time in the home. Fathers might tell you that you are trying to feminize men with all this nurturing. Or, unruly participants might test you by disrupting the group in other ways. You need to lovingly stand your ground, defend the vision of nurturing men and maintain the integrity of the group. Ironically, sensitivity is one of the values we are trying to inculcate in modern men; yet if this quality is displayed excessively you may lose some of your ability to make your argument.

Benefits of an Elevated Vision

Keep in mind that I'm not talking about actual physical battle. The Warrior must be ready to engage in a tactical verbal and metaphysical exchange, not shying away from conflict because peacefulness at any cost is seen as a higher virtue than being confrontive or decisive. I'd like to remind readers that two of the greatest peacemakers of the last century were also two of the biggest Warriors: Mahatma Gandhi and Martin Luther King, Jr. Both men had a powerful vision that was at odds with the status quo, and many well-intended observers suggested that they let their struggle go as it was seemingly creating more tension. But when you are a social change agent, you don't ignore injustice in your area of influence. When you sign up to be a fathers' group facilitator, you become a social change agent. Whether those who dismiss your work are in your group or outside of it, you must be willing to stand up for a new model of fatherhood and manhood.

The successful Warrior has an elevated vision that he leads his comrades toward. This is a quest that he must use his determination and power to complete. The group facilitator acquires a degree of power and prestige. It is important not to use it in vain, ego inspired debacles. The momentum of the group may carry you forward with more force then you realize even if you find yourself traveling down the wrong road.

One goal of a well run fathers' group is to awaken the inner archetypes of the participants. Yes, you may serve as a guide, but only until their own intuition and reason has developed to a sufficient degree that they can read the road signs and trust their own internal guidance. That's not to imply participants will not need the group if they are emotionally mature, spiritually awake individuals. More evolved men may come to the group because they know the group is healing and helps to maintain their equilibrium and balance. They understand the need to strengthen their inner

Warrior (or other archetypes) and they understand that your group environment is beneficial.

The Warrior protects you and the group as it moves away from what is known and familiar toward a new ethic, with new ideas and new social norms. This journey heralds a new stage of life. Sometimes the determination of your participants to complete the journey weakens and they decide that where they are is not so bad. They no longer feel like putting the effort into completing the journey and can't remember why they started this stupid trip to begin with. They may start to belittle the journey and its destination. The facilitator as Warrior makes sure participants don't wander too far off course as that could endanger the journey for themselves and other participants.

Facilitator Example

"Don't bring weapons to the group," was one of the implied rules. We didn't spell it out on the list of group rules during the first session. It was imbedded in the "Show respect to others" and "Accept differences of opinion" and others. A participant might argue that bringing a knife or gun to the group wasn't disrespectful as long as he didn't threaten any other participants with it. But I saw it as an unspoken rule, and I was surprised when Tyrone stood up for the meal break in the middle of one session and I observed a steak knife drop from his jacket. We had never had steak for dinner during the group before and I felt Tyrone knew it was not on the menu that evening, so he had to have brought the knife for another reason. Tyrone looked up at me, a little surprised and embarrassed as the brown plastic handle and serrated metal edges bounced lightly on the carpeted floor.

Two other dads were still in the room and saw the knife fall, too. Their eyes quickly met mine, confirming that they had seen the knife. They looked more amused than frightened and in a few accelerated heartbeats all three of them were out of the room. I was left with a dilemma. I was pretty confident the knife was not intended to threaten or hurt any man in our group. I might have waited to talk with Tyrone after the group if the other two guys had not seen it, but he had compromised the integrity of the group and we all knew it. His sheepishness when he picked up the knife confirmed he knew it as well. If I let it slide, an undercurrent of dis-ease would begin to percolate through the group. Soon people might start to feel uncomfortable and pack their own defenses or simply stop coming. The group is a sanctuary, a haven. Even if our sessions are in the midst of an urban battleground, it's understood to be a violence-free zone.

So The Warrior facilitator did what had to be done. I went to my brother and asked to talk to him outside. I could peep the other guys who had seen the knife watching us. The important thing to remember about The Warrior is that he excels in compassionate confrontation.

I said, "Tyrone, you know you're not supposed to have weapons in the group."

Tyrone accepted the implied rule without question. "I know, but I didn't bring it 'cause I had beef with no one in the group. It's just to keep me safe walking from the station to my house."

"That's what I thought, and I don't want to put you in danger. But it sends out the wrong message for you to have it during the group—especially since it dropped on the floor like that where everyone can see it. You might think of a safer way to carry it so it's not dropping on the floor at the wrong moments. Can I hold it and give it back to you at the end of group?"

"Okay, I'm sorry, Haji. Here, you can have it now and I won't bring it again. I'll figure out something else to do with it."

I appreciated him solving my dilemma about what to do about the knife during future sessions. I recognize we live in a violent society and many of the men who participate in our groups are at risk of community violence. I was serious about not wanting to put Tyrone at greater risk and would have worked with him to figure out a way to feel safer in transit, even if it meant me dropping him home after the group. The important thing was addressing the infraction with him. Feeling the fear and doing it anyway.

I once heard a community activist talk about the broken window syndrome. If there's one broken window in a neighborhood, it starts to send the message that the residents don't care about the community and pretty soon a bigger and bigger assortment of problems start to plague the neighborhood—all because the initial, minor violation of a broken window wasn't dealt with. It's similar with small infractions in the group. Send The Warrior out to deal with these immediately and they won't grow into bigger issues.

Participant Example

Participant Examples of The Warrior look a little different from some of the other archetypes because if you are fulfilling your role as The Warrior facilitator, participants need do little more than have your back in terms of group dynamic, but you may hear of them defending the group in other spheres of their life.

There was one young brother named Tony who came to a group at his child's preschool. He was a late 20s dad who still hung around with "his boys" a lot. From the way he described them, you could tell their opinions were pretty important to him and he shared a lot of values with them. But a funny thing started to happen as he attended the group week after week. His loyalty seemed to slightly shift away from the guys he had been hanging out with and become more aligned with his new peer group in the fathers' group.

It was almost imperceptible at first and it never became so polarized that he had to renounce his old network. But at our graduation I was happy to hear that Tony had invoked The Warrior to defend our group against subtle attack.

He said, "You know, when I first started coming to this group my friends used to tease me. 'Oh, Tony, can't come out, he's got to go to his *father's group*. And stuff like that.' At first, it didn't bother me cause I wasn't sure what I was gonna get out of it or if I was even gonna continue. But after awhile, I really started to enjoy it and I would tell 'em to back off, this is good for me. Shoot, I told the ones that were dads they needed to come with me so they could be better fathers!"

You may not always see when participants defend the honor of the group, but if they keep coming you will certainly feel their allegiance and you should trust that carving out time in their busy schedule to participant is one basic and primary way that they defend the group.

Shadow

The Warrior has a strong Shadow. In my mind, there is a distinction between The Warrior and a soldier. The soldier is more of a hired gun, even if it's by his own government. The Warrior is a more of a self-directed agent. However, even The Warrior has a way of running roughshod over the more delicate aspects of the journey and you need to guard against this. Especially with a group of men you, as group facilitator, need to remain vigilant about incorporating the intuition of The Mystic, the nurturance of The Mother Hen, and the heart centeredness of The Lover to guide your vision. Men love The Warrior's energy and don't always want to seek direction from the quieter elements of our nature, but this is what a successful Warrior does. Learning to listen to both the harder and softer aspects of your facilitator personality is key to a successful job.

It's easy for a facilitator to become so engrossed with his map that he fails to see the terrain that he is traveling through. This, however, is one of the most important elements of the journey. A facilitator who chooses to listen to the voice of his ego rather than his conscience is going to cut people off, seem bombastic and generally overreact to any infraction, real or imagined. This is a dangerous foundation of power for The Warrior. The same skills you model in the group are the skills that you encourage your participants to model with their families.

We facilitators want fathers not to be so dependent on their ego and instead try to hear the quieter voice of their conscience when it speaks in relationship to their children and co-parent. The ego always wants to be right. It wants to forcibly roll over other family members. He believes his authority as a father gives him permission not to listen. By demonstrating a more egalitarian model of leadership you show the men in the group how they can listen and empathize, and you still can lead the group where you know it needs to go. If you allow the enforcer energy of the group to come from a shallow place, you will undermine a lot of the good that the group could do. After all, The Warrior has the responsibility not only to protect, but also to guide and serve.

Recommendations

1. Internalize the groups' vision and norms in your own thoughts; that way, you will quickly become aware of disruptions from other people or yourself and able to respond from a place of compassion. Keep the goal of enlightened relationships in the crosshairs of your movement forward. Many diversions will emerge on the road to success and if you don't remain aware, you may find yourself racing toward an inhospitable place.
2. A lot is at stake with each interaction. With great power comes great responsibility. Warriors are slow to anger and use their emotions to motivate them toward their real goal, not to get distracted by drama. Stay in tune with the other archetypes so that your internal GPS can help you steer away from potential hazards. At the same time, remember it is your task to maintain the integrity and safety of the group. Don't shy away from conflict because you're afraid. Feel the fear and do the right thing, anyway.

Power Question

There will be many challenges to your leadership as you facilitate an emotionally charged group based on participants making sometimes drastic changes in their attitudes and behaviors.

The Warrior asks:

How do you protect the group and keep it moving forward?

9 The Juggler

Affirmation

I am attentive, coordinated and calm.

Description

The Juggler is known for his ability to keep an impressive number of balls in the air while remaining focused and relaxed. This is an essential skill for running a fathers' group. Not only do you have a dozen men, more or less, in the room who are all seeking your attention, but each one wants you to orchestrate the scene so that all the other dads in the room understand how important he is. Thus, there are the many layers of interaction happening simultaneously which you will have to remain aware of.

For example, at any given moment, several men can be experiencing sadness that their father abandoned them in some way; a few more are feeling angry at how their girlfriends treated them earlier in the day. Another is worried about his son having problems in school and the school staff's recent suggestion that he go on medication. Another man can't focus on the discussion because he's worried about where money for food is coming from this week.

As you facilitate, you're wondering why two guys who said they were coming last night didn't show up, plus you're watching the clock to make sure you stay on time to move on to the next activity, and you're wondering what you can cut from the session because it looks like you're going over time.

Welcome to The Juggler! When we think about facilitation, in many ways, The Juggler is the core archetype. You can imagine him keeping tracking of and dealing with all the other archetypes, seamlessly transitioning between The Mystic, The Salesman and The CEO. Due to the extensive practice he's logged, The Juggler makes his task look easy. This underlines the need to learn the fundamentals of facilitation. You will not get good facilitation gigs until you get some experience, but how do you get experience facilitating groups? You remain aware when you are in groups during all the other situations in your life. Your family of origin is a group, your current family is a group, your work colleagues are a group, your crew of friends is a group. Human beings are social animals and when you think about it we are often in groups; if you use those as learning/practicing opportunities, you will gain skills as a facilitator.

Benefits of Relaxed Awareness

The goal of a good fathers' group is to help each man improve his skills as a healthy human who can guide others toward a place of maturity and responsibility. Once you accept the role of facilitating this kind of experience, it is hard to return to an unaware standpoint with all the other groups you belong to. You naturally begin to look for opportunities to help other groups embody the dynamic growth that your fathers' group enjoys. You begin looking for ways to embody the positive archetypes we are discussing in this book to advocate for social change in whatever arena you find yourself. Your practice of The Juggler becomes pervasive.

The fundamental skill of The Juggler involves *relaxed awareness.* There is always much activity happening on many different levels of a men's group. On one end of the spectrum, the Juggler feigns unawareness of the multi-dimensional nature of the interactions in his group (I say feigns because on a deeper level, he is aware of it), and he just deals with the most superficial element of who is speaking now. On the other end of the spectrum, The Juggler tries to stay aware of the 35 separate interactions which are happening during every instant of a group session. Unable to process that much information, he glides to the other end of the spectrum, dealing with only the most superficial aspects of the group until he's ready to expand his awareness again.

The trick is to stay on the middle path, relaxed awareness. If The Juggler can think about the two men who said they were coming but have not arrived while simultaneously moving on to the session's next segment, he keeps the balls in the air. If The Juggler can connect the body language of participants who are looking anxious with the back story that he has gleaned from each man and connect those pieces during the session, he keeps the balls in the air. If The Juggler can remember one participant's angst about his son or daughter's reports from school while another participant speaks he may be able to connect a dad to a parenting practice that will help him—and he keeps the balls in the air.

This ability to entertain a thought and then move on takes mental, spiritual and emotional practice. The meditative ability to scan your thoughts without becoming attached to them is a skill that, once you become proficient, will pay off enormously in all areas of your life, as juggling is a fundamental skill required of all mature adults, especially those who facilitate groups.

Facilitator Example

The Juggler is one of the most prolific of all the archetypes present in excellent facilitation. Dozens of examples will occur over a single session of facilitation. I'll break out a concrete example now.

During a recent group session I was sitting in a circle of men in an oddly shaped room. We were in the midst of a discussion from the curriculum about practices that constitute a healthy relationship between parents. I knew that at least two of the nine men had been so traumatized by the mothers of their children they were not open to any kind of intimacy with a female. So, those two, at best, were having only superficial relationships with women, with the exception of their babies' mothers and these were was highly conflictual. Four of the men, including me, were married with varying degrees of success, and the other four men were somewhere in between. Keeping this wide spectrum of interests in mind as we discussed the topic constitutes several balls in the air right there.

In addition, the child care person was feeling overwhelmed because a four-year-old boy (why it is always a boy?) had been giving her a hard time the last few weeks and I was on notice that his father might have to be called to speak to him. As I was trying to float these factors in my consciousness, the caterer walked in early wanting to know where we wanted the food and who had his money. It's never a good idea to keep the group waiting too long to get their food, but we were in the middle of a good discussion. I decided to start wrapping up the first part of the group, let guys eat, bring the kids down for food, check in with one of the dads who had reported having a car accident earlier in the week and continue planning the second half of the group in my head.

You get it. It doesn't stop. You have to keep moving and not get paralyzed by the energy.

And, finally, right before the break, one of the guys who was missing walked in and his first words were, "Didn't you get my message?" No, I apologized. I try to keep my cell phone loud and close by before groups in case someone tries to get me, but sometimes I forget. The Juggler will drop balls sometimes. Michael Jordan missed shots sometimes.

To be one of the best, you don't have to be perfect. You just have to be in the game and be better than most people. Cooperation, not competition, is one of the hallmarks of the new masculine ethic. But it would be insincere not to acknowledge a hierarchy of facilitation professionals in any region big enough to support more than one dads' group. Ultimately, you are competing against your own best game. But as your best game improves, other players will begin to notice – and that's a good feeling.

Participant Example

The Juggler is a great example of how participants model the archetypes we're discussing both in and out of the fathers' group. Clearly, any involved parent must be a great Juggler, or multi-tasker, as the modern image projects. A major reason why many men will resist your Salesman pitch is because they feel they have too much stuff going on at work and home to add another commitment to their busy lives. Even if you can demonstrate to them how participating in the group will increase their overall work/life balance and satisfaction, you will still undoubtedly be sitting in a circle with a dozen men thinking of dozens of different scenarios throughout the time of each group.

Some of their concerns can be dropped in the middle of the circle and will lighten their load immediately. Some of their concerns, however, will seem too private or inconsequential to share and the dads will be ruminating on those topics as you facilitate the group. The dads will naturally slip into thinking about what happened during their day at work, what's the agenda for when they get home after the group and the big scary thought that worries them at odd hours of the day and night. By demonstrating The Juggler with aplomb, you role model for your dads how to keep all their balls securely and comfortably up in the air.

When dads come to the group stressed because they have too much going on in their lives, the group becomes a refuge or sanctuary. Participants may realize they can comfortably put down several balls and still be a nurturing dad. Maybe they realize they weren't, in fact, juggling many balls but instead were playing catch with one mega-ball called "salary." By being in the group, they are reminded to diversify and pick up the "playing with the kids" ball, or "helping with homework" ball. Being in the group may not minimize the number of balls that participants have in the air, but it will help them to reprioritize tasks and responsibilities so they can gain more overall satisfaction with their life.

Shadow

The Juggler is such a pervasive archetype that his Shadow has become equally common: it's known as Attention Deficient Syndrome, or ADD. When there are so many separate issues vying for your attention, it's impossible not to have your attention split somewhat. Cooking and thinking of what the kids are watching in the next room. Sitting in your cubicle at work, trying to focus on one project and thinking of the three other ones you need to start on as soon as this one is over. Finally, you get some quiet time with the one you love and you find yourself thinking of the cute girl at work. A divided mind is a dull tool to take into the workplace of modern life. The Juggler's Shadow can be illustrated by the image of a garden hose with many large pinpricks along the length of the hose. The Juggler is holding the nozzle of the hose over his garden, wondering why just a trickle of water comes out and as he goes to look for the problem, he discovers dozens of small holes that cause the water pressure to diminish before it reaches its goal. That's the problem you're dealing with when you have too many balls with no sense of priority.

Practicing The Juggler's affirmation to be attentive, calm and coordinated is what minimizes the Shadow. As we've pointed out, there will always be an array of issues to focus on and you must be able to scan and prioritize them to be grounded. For some people, keeping lists of what they need to do or focus on relieves much of the stress of performing. You just need to check your list. Facilitators who wind up dropping the ball often lack the ability to quickly and effectively scan. If you are obsessing over one single aspect of nurturing, do what you can (maybe simply writing down a future action) and then move on. Spacing out and giving up are often symptoms of simply being too tired. This can be physical tiredness or mental tiredness. Make sure to nurture yourself. Get plenty of rest and prioritize to avoid being overcome by The Juggler's Shadow.

Recommendations

1. Because The Juggler is such an essential archetype, it is important to maintain awareness of his central role. When you are starting to feel overwhelmed by the tremendous number of conflicting activities that are required in your role as facilitator, relax. This is normal. Do a quick mental scan of what you have coming down the road, immediate and long-term, and then focus on the priority you can do best right now. Put the other activities out of your mind until you are required to think about them. Use your breath and your self-talk to deliberately calm yourself down while simultaneously focusing on your immediate task and keeping an eye on the big picture.

2. Practice and planning make The Juggler dramatically more efficient in his role. If you send an adequate amount of time prepping the time frame for each group and planning for "unforeseen" occurrences that may arise, it's much less likely you will be caught unaware. Know the various roles you are required to play and think of those who can help you beforehand, or what you can do yourself before you head into the group when the intensity will be highest. Guard against the debilitating effects of ADD by letting go of challenges you cannot manage at this moment in time; write a note to come back to them during your planning process. Most of all, pay attention to all the fathers who sit in your circle and what you can do during each session to serve them because that is how you will build the strongest bond and rapport. Let extraneous pulls on your time go.

Power Question

The Juggler is required to maintain awareness of many competing interests vying for his attention. In quieter times, The Juggler needs to look at all the components of running a group and ask himself: How do I keep all the balls in the air?

10 The Recluse

Affirmation

I enjoy myself while I am alone.

Description

It may seem like I say this about all the archetypes, but The Recluse is one of my favorites. This may even seem like an odd archetype to be included in a book on group facilitation, but it is truly one of the most important. In the context of group facilitation, The Recluse represents not only balance, but also a necessary contrast. The Recluse, for the group facilitator, represents the exhalation that must accompany every inhalation. Leading a group is like inhaling a breath; it's like being on stage. Time in solitude, represented by The Recluse, is like exhaling. It's a necessary balance for the group leader.

When you facilitate, you perform in front of a crowd even though a master group facilitator looks like he is doing little because everyone in the group takes ownership when sessions are done well. This requires a massive series of behind the scenes actions. Not only do you make sure the room is set up, the food arrives on time and you know your session content, but more so, you make sure that everyone gets a chance to be heard; that deep, unspoken feelings are voiced; and most of all, that everyone feels safe to be vulnerable. In order to execute these varied and crucial tasks in an understated manner so people do not feel controlled or manipulated, the group facilitator must have achieved a certain level of self-mastery or self-realization and that achievement is never earned on the stage of the world.

To facilitate an excellent fathers' group requires integrity. You must have integrated the discordant aspects of your own personality enough that you can lead other men in a good, orderly direction. You can't successfully run a fathers' group while your life is in chaos. We all have road bumps and often the biggest problems teach us the most important lessons. In order to grasp those lessons, you usually need to slow down and integrate the problem experience into your overall sense of well-being. That requires self-reflection and might take a few days or a few years. There are many methods that help you do this. All of them connect you with your higher self. And they each demand the discipline to develop a certain level of confidence before you ever try to recruit the first participant.

Benefits of Mind-Body Practice

For me, yoga, meditation, reading, and being in healthy relationships are key methods I use to prepare myself for facilitating groups. The first method is optional; most of the other great fathers' group facilitators I know do not do yoga, except in the broadest definition of the word (i.e., union with the Supreme). Any sort of mind-body practice would apply here: regular gym workouts, running, a physical team sport. The key here is that you are a reasonably healthy person in a physical and mental sense. Although it's mostly sedentary, journaling is another excellent way to build self-aware-ness. I know of no great fathers' group facilitators who are grossly unhealthy in their appearance or attitude. Successful facilitators will have something positive beyond parenting skills to share about what it means to be a man. Obviously, this must include our physical manifestation.

Yoga has a profound spiritual sensibility linked to physical activity (at least in terms of the most popular yoga in the West, Hatha Yoga; many other paths of yoga are less body-focused than the various forms of Hatha Yoga which have blossomed so vibrantly in the U.S.). Many successful dads' group leaders I know have a deeply developed religious or spiritual life. While not a prerequisite, this type of work tends to attract people who are compassionate and want to serve their communities. So any prayer, reflective practice or devotional reading you pursue during your Recluse times will serve you well in the group. The Recluse is really about going within to activate your inner light or your higher power, so you can come back and share it with the world at a later time, especially during your group work.

This balance of inner work combined with outer work is one of the keys to running a great group. You need to equally develop the extroverted and introverted aspects of your personality. No matter which side of the spectrum you start on, you will have to strengthen the corresponding opposite. Participants in the groups I facilitate don't realize how introverted I can be. I would be very happy in a secluded house in the woods or desert for quite a long time. With nothing but books, a word processor and Mother Nature, I could make myself content without other human contact for weeks.

I throw myself into these groups because I also genuinely love people and I see how we are all connected. I am convinced that small group work (eight to 18 people) is essential to the health of our society. We are too disconnected from one another, fragmented within ourselves and lacking in connection to others, for conscious folks to sit on the sidelines. From working on myself I became convinced I had something to share and was happy I found this format which is so powerful. So I push myself to reach out to others and find I am energized by the connections.

On the other hand, maybe you are someone who's a natural extrovert. You're great at talking to people about the group. You have no problem getting folks excited to attend and maybe you can even keep folks coming out, but you sense that the depth of experience I'm describing does not happen in your group. It's more like people are *attending* your show than *participating* in an experience. A high level of sharing, disclosure, and vulnerability on the part of participants is not happening. Maybe you need to be a little less extroverted. Maybe your personality is too big and you need tone it down a bit so other men will—energetically—have a space to come into.

The feeling that we have to do everything is a serious problem with a lot of leaders. But in facilitating a fathers' group you <u>cannot</u> do everything. You must allow space for the participants to grow and shine and that means you must pull back. If you're a serious extrovert, as a lot of people who aspire to lead groups will naturally be, you may not even know you have this problem. One of the best ways to assess your energetic influence on the group is in quiet, solo reflection, where your higher self can point out situations where there was too much of you. Sitting in meditation, going for a long run, practicing martial arts, anything that quiets your chatty mind will help point out ways you can create more space for other men to be present in the group. It's crucial for you to give yourself downtime to assess this need.

Depending on where you are in your journey you may need more or less time to develop this awareness, but you should always maintain some time to recharge your batteries away from the demands of the group and your own family. The Recluse is a good archetype to invoke when considering healthy boundaries with your group participants. Participants will need attention outside of the group. Assessments should be done, crises must be managed, relationships need cultivation. But there will be men who are not able to respect your personal space—not the three-foot physical space rule, the more subtle psychic space rule. These men will call you at inappropriate times, make inappropriate requests and generally try to cannibalize your energy. You must be able to tell these folks no. You don't need an elaborate subterfuge; you don't need to invent excuses about going out with friends. You are enough. You need to work on yourself in solitude. You need to be The Recluse and benefit accordingly.

Some group leaders become co-dependent with overly needy men because they are afraid of themselves. They do not like to be alone with their own thoughts and foibles. Some men are constantly running around putting out fires and slaying demons outside their skin, when their biggest enemy lurks between their ears. What do you do when you're alone? Are you always wasting time on the Internet, in front of the TV, or getting high? Do you feel that running off to answer every crisis call is more important than cultivating your inner life? Are you even aware that you have an inner life?

Facilitating a well run fathers' group will bring up a lot of buried "stuff" from your own life. If you've been successfully dealing with it before starting the group you understand The Recluse somewhat already. But if you have been running from your own stuff, from your own demons, you have been running from The Recluse. If so, this chapter may seem frightening or ridiculous to you. But in order for you to successfully lead a group, you need to successfully be alone. They are two sides of the same coin, like the inhalation and the exhalation.

So take the time to develop your inner practice; it need not be complicated or consume huge portions of your day. It does require some discipline and consistency. You may get to the point where you love your reflective activities as much as you love the excitement of the group.

Facilitator Example

During the pre-group assessment, Rob and I hit it off. He was a couple of years older than me, but we grew up in the same neighborhood, listened to the same music and both started using the same drugs as teenagers. I stayed mostly with weed and he went mostly toward alcohol so when our addictions got out of control, they went in different directions. He became homeless several times and started using whatever drugs he could get his hands on. Eventually he got clean in prison doing a bid for armed robbery. When he came out he found religion and reconnected with his children. Nice guy, but he wanted to be friends too hard with me.

After every group, Rob wanted to hang out and talk with me. During the first several weeks, when I called every participant the night before group to remind them, Rob was always the hardest one to get off the phone with. He asked so many questions about my wife and kids, it started creeping me out. Then he started inviting me over to his house to hang out. I've become friends with men that are participants in groups I facilitate, but I didn't like Rob like that. He was a fine group member, but he wasn't the kind of guy I wanted to hang out with. In fact, I preferred my own company and that's what I told him:

> "Sorry, Bro, I can't come by, I need to get some work done. I need to catch up on some reading and writing and just spend some downtime with my family."

I was worried that Rob might drop out of the group when I didn't give him more attention, but he got all the attention he deserved—from me. Eventually, he got it and settled into being a good group member without having to be my best friend. If I hadn't been willing to stand up for my right to have my own self-reflective downtime, I surely would have gotten resentful toward Rob. As it was, I was able to show empathy and maintain a clear boundary, both essential characteristics for building strong relationships. And he understood.

Participant Example

A participant with a healthy degree of The Recluse will be indistinguishable from any other participant. His extroverted side comes to the fore during group and in his comments you hear he takes appropriate time for self-reflection outside of the group. A participant who's leaning too heavily toward The Recluse side, however, may exclude himself from connecting with the other men. This can set up an awkward dynamic in the group because you have a man who sets up a vacuum in the middle of your circle. His presence may short-circuit the energy around him.

Jonathan was one such man. His outward appearance wasn't very different from the other men in the group. He was in his late 30s, almond colored skin, on the short, stocky side with a short afro. He usually wore dark blue work pants and shirt, but he was mostly unemployed. There was an intense hostility emanating from him. All his family stories were depressing when you could get him to talk and that was like pulling teeth. He had been raised in foster care and now lived in a rooming house. He claimed his foster parents disliked him and vice versa. The mother of his one child didn't want anything to do with him and, frankly, I could understand why. Jonathan was a downer.

That he was depressed was not a mystery. He only came to my group because I pursued him by phone beyond what any other professional had done. He seemed to enjoy the attention. With my overwhelming belief in the power of the group process and the potential create a better relationship with his daughter, I persuaded him to come. He spread negative vibes over the group for a month and a half. He was never friendly toward any of the other men; he kept to himself during breaks and told stories of loneliness and abandonment when he did share. His was a heavy presence.

Again, I emphasize a healthy degree of The Recluse in a participant is hard to distinguish in the group because he will interact appropriately with the other dads. One difference is you will hear him talking about taking down time for himself. A healthy Recluse is not a gloomy figure; this brother was deep into The Recluse Shadow.

Through the power of the group, however, Jonathan did have a catharsis and his demeanor changed. He began to balance The Recluse with other archetypes. While he never became the belle of the ball, he did become friendlier with the other men and it seemed like being alive was less of a burden on him. In a relatively short three-month period of time, you can't expect an entire personality to change. The important thing to remember with The Recluse participant is to keep drawing him out and know he attends the group to achieve what he may only subconsciously desire: greater balance and equilibrium in his life.

Shadow

We've touched a bit on The Recluse Shadow in the participant description. This is one that can get real deep and hard to penetrate. Not that all recluses are depressed, in some cases, seclusion can be a healthy response to toxic environments. However, researchers are learning more about how men display depression differently than women and it may be that a lot of this strong, silent man type bravado is actually depression in disguise. To have healthy relationships one needs to be able to both express empathy and maintain boundaries. Fully participating in a fathers' group can be the deepest form of healing empathy and intimacy that many men have experienced outside of a sexual relationship. For some men, even sexual relationships have not been as emotionally connecting as what they experience in a good fathers' group! Guys like Jonathan who are very deep into The Recluse Shadow may utterly resist your appeals to join in group sessions where something like openness and awareness may emerge.

Most guys who are inclined to attend groups will likely have a more subtle Recluse Shadow than Jonathan. Our society does not promote a lot of places where men can really join with other men. Either playing or watching sports or engaging in workplace social life or the bar scene are some of the few opportunities. Fathers' groups are healthy, competition- and judgment-reduced (if not competition- and judgment-free) spaces where men can begin to drop their masks, relax their boundaries and build empathic relationships with other humans who are not sexual partners or blood kin. It's great practice for other areas of life.

Those drawn to facilitation tend to be so outgoing, we may have less of a tendency toward deep, dangerous reclusiveness. But it helps to be aware of the characteristics in our own lives as well as with those in groups with us. It's important to build downtime into our schedules and fill it up with life enhancing activities.

Recommendations

1. Spend some time alone in quiet reflection both to prepare for and debrief from your group. The insights that will come to you about the participants in your group and how you should roll during each session can be amazing when you take time to reflect quietly on your mission before and after the group! It may also be necessary, of course, to prepare and debrief with others whom you respect and work with, but remember to hold fast to your own counsel.
2. Do something meaningful with your "downtime." Create some rituals that you enjoy and look forward to. Spent time in prayer and meditation, read good books, interact with your inner child. During sessions you should model and talk about your personal development activities as the men in your group see you as their leader and are inclined to follow your example.

Power Question

This question will help to distinguish healthy alone time from toxic alone time. The enlightened Recluse asks:

How do you enjoy yourself when alone?

11 The Gambler

Affirmation

I am lucky.

Description

The Gambler helps to keep the group exciting! The Gambler brings a sense of adventure and daring to the group, ensures that leaps in awareness take place when necessary and that boredom doesn't take over your group. If you use one of the well designed fathers' groups' curriculum that is available, you'll have a great jumping off point from which to use The Gambler. Even though these curricula have many similar activities, the people that populate the group make each cycle unique and combined with your willingness to take healthy risks in pursuit of individual and group progress, this keeps each group fresh.

The Gambler's role is to evaluate the chance for success when a risky facilitation opportunity presents itself and have the courage to pull the trigger on a risky proposition when success is deemed probable. The stakes are high, up to and including, relationship stability and in extreme cases, life or death. Because of this, The

Gambler needs to be activated with extreme caution. When you are not sure what a dad's reaction will be to a risky question or suggestion, or if you yourself are unsure about the possible ramifications, it's better to leave The Gambler alone. However, there are times when your gut tells you that you've got to take this risk, the rewards are too high to ignore and the possible downside is manageable. It's then that you must have the courage to go for it and take the gamble.

So, what kind of risk and gamble are we talking about here? You're really gambling with people's awareness, including your own. We all live in our own little tunnel vision versions of reality and by doing group work like this you are betting that the men who attend will expand their point of view to include healthier relationship paradigms. What's the point of doing intensive self-study if you remain the same? Since everyone has blind spots in their awareness and nobody likes to have their personal beliefs challenged, there's always some risk involved in questioning the tunnel version of reality that participants walk in with. Sometimes participants are able to see their blind spot or sense the obsolescence of a personal (or group-based) belief, and sometimes they are not.

The risk and gamble begins when you are recruiting. At that point, you have a lot to lose and the men very little. They have no investment in you or your group. You're gambling when you approach every single man or each time you pick up the phone to recruit. And in a few minutes, you've got to create enough leverage that this guy will rearrange his life to attend your group. That's a gamble. Do your job as The Salesman well and a father will bet along with you that there's something beneficial that he can take out of his time in your group. Now, he's put a wager of his time on the table and you're both gambling something.

Benefits of Insight

As the group sessions continue, The Gambler facilitator needs to take bigger, more well thought out risks. Just maintaining order in the group requires something of a gamble. You need to constantly assess your relationship with each guy and how much you can push him. For instance, the group rules state participants need to come on time and be respectful of other men in the group. If someone is constantly late, argues with the other men, but still brings a lot of energy to the group, you've got to get him to follow group discipline him even if you risk him leaving the group. The Gambler takes a risk on losing other participants if he's unable to uphold the norms of the group. This archetype will need to assess how much he can push a man in the group to help the dad see how one of his blind spots is causing harm to his relationships.

More poignantly, The Gambler needs to assess his own blind spots, or have access to a method that will help him do this (such as a co-facilitator or someone he trusts to conduct debriefings). Just because you can see a blind spot in someone else doesn't mean you don't have them yourself. Many of us are more insightful when it comes to other people's limitations than when dealing with our own. That's why some of the other archetypes ask you to reflect on your own blind spots and the better you get at identifying and eliminating them, the better stories you will have to share with your participants about how men change.

Generally, this archetype is kept in storage during the early weeks of the group because you are still developing a strong connection with the men. Again, your observations and suggestions for change in the men may stir up deeply rooted conflict. If a guy jokes about watching porn, The Gambler may not seriously challenge his viewing habits right out of the box. You look at the hand you're dealt, assess cards he and the other men are holding around porn. What are people's attitudes? How has it affected their families? Gain more information.

At some point, The Gambler points out some of the damaging effects of using porn, how it can desensitize men to sex with their partners, how they can talk to their children about the pornification of our culture. At some point in the conversations, you'll want to challenge men to look at their behavior. Same thing with substance abuse, fear of intimacy, depression, and other emotional issues. While you see that it is a gamble to bring up behaviors that men in your group may not want to talk about, raising the issue may be the crux of the change they need to make to be the men they want to be. It's a delicate dance. Gamble too much, too soon, you lose them; don't gamble enough, soon enough and no one changes.

Like all good facilitation, there is both science and art in this. You know you are going to have to confront difficult topics with people. A good curriculum will guide you through the topics you need to discuss. But every participant may not be ready to discuss the downside of using corporal punishment in week six. He's had 30 years of encouragement to use physical discipline and when you bring up some of the other methods it feels soft and ineffective to him. Pushing that man too hard in week six may be too high a risk. The Gambler stores that information away, like counting cards in a game of blackjack, and when he sees all the aces exhausted from the deck, he knows he can safely play his hand. That's how The Gambler works.

Facilitator Example

Anytime you observe or hear about a change in a brother's behavior, you can chalk it up to The Gambler at work, even going back to the most rudimentary gamble of inviting each man to the group. Often, The Gambler operates gradually and is so subtle that over time, it's hard to discern exactly when he's present. The Gambler usually appears with the thought, *Should I say this to this guy?* It's appropriate that The Gambler often appears with a questioning thought because it is often best to invoke him in the form of a question.

During one series I had this very provocative dad in my group. He was charismatic and a leader in his own right, but he came from a very traditional background in terms of what was appropriate for men and women to do in the home. Like many of us he was conflicted about the changing roles of fathers and accepted some aspects of the new paradigm with enthusiasm, but was not comfortable with other corresponding parts. For example, he said he had no problem staying home and taking care of his kids since their mother had a job that made more money than he was able to. But he called her frequently and tried to be very controlling when she was out which made it difficult for her to be successful in her job. This made him less successful as a stay-at-home dad, especially since it seemed like he saved much of the parenting and housework for her to do when she came home.

One night we were talking about dividing up parenting tasks and he mentioned he was upset that his wife complained that he could do more to clean the house when he was at home. He told us he was busy with the kids all day and felt like that was her job.

> I knew there were issues of masculinity at stake since he had come from a pretty traditional background in terms of gender, but I felt The Gambler push so I asked him, "How much would you expect her to clean if roles were reversed and she was home with the kids all day?"

"I would expect her to keep the house clean if I was out all day."

"So, why is it different for you?"

If I had been gambling on a slot machine, his expression would have been three cherries. He started to say something, but then stopped and his mouth hung open a little as all the energy seeped from his body. It was obvious whatever he was about to say was so repugnant to even himself that he couldn't push it out. All the guys in the group laughed out loud, and he sensed the laughter was innocent; we were all laughing at our own prejudiced expectations about women and culture.

I sealed the deal by saying, "Maybe you want to think about picking up a few more things while she's at work?"

He was honest enough to say, "Yeah, maybe I will."

And I was cautious enough to save the risk of confronting him about the frequent calls for another evening.

Participant Example

The participant as Gambler happens in two ways: in the group and at home. It's great for dads to take chances in the group, to try on new attitudes and behaviors and then take those new skills home and try them with their family. That is a gamble. For guys that may not have been very involved with their kids to take them out to the park alone, or to make suggestions to their mother that the family try a new discipline technique, these are gambles that dads need some courage to take. Like the facilitator seeking men to even attend the group, they are taking a risk. They are gambling. If you run a good group, they will continue coming. They will see the risk pay off and will be open to more gambles in the future.

One dad in particular exemplifies this for me. This brother, Donald, was referred by the state child welfare organization and he did not want to attend. I believe even those who are mandated by the courts can get a lot from attending a group because the energy is so high. Donald was not a true believer in the beginning. His gamble was based on the equation that attending the group was a better bet than losing his kids or having his kids' mother pissed at him for not doing what the Department of Children and Families ordered. He came to a group that started in January; big puffy South Pole jackets were popular at this time. For the first three weeks, Donald did not take off his South Pole inside the circle in a well heated room. He rarely uncrossed his arms, he never said a word unless prompted and then he was monosyllabic.

But the gamble that brought Donald to the fathers' group paid big dividends. After the first few weeks, Donald started opening up his coat and his mouth. His demeanor softened, he talked more often about the conflicts and tension in his home, and he started trying some of the strategies that were suggested to him for solving some common family problems. By the time graduation came around, Donald was clearly happy that he'd gambled on coming to the group.

Shadow

The two great dangers with The Gambler are overreach and overcaution. You know that gambling can be an addictive behavior and I know for a facilitator The Gambler temptation can get really strong as well. In a group situation, you're obviously not gambling with money, you're gambling with emotions and awareness, which can be even more volatile than gambling with cash. What you will lose by making bets that are not well thought out is not money, but men.

If you find a lot of guys are not returning to your group, it could be because they find it too boring or it might be because they find it too dangerous. It feels dangerous to be in a group where the facilitator is too risk friendly. It feels like every session will feature several men being dramatically confronted over some perceived fault in their parenting. While that may make for exciting fireworks in the group, the men who are confronted without establishing a strong bond first will feel violated and the men who witnessed the violation will wonder when it will be their turn. They will make silent plans not to be around when that happens.

It takes a certain degree of intuition and confidence to determine when it's appropriate to use The Gambler. If you challenge every dad on every limit every week, you won't have time to follow the curriculum and you'll set up a hostile learning environment. The true Gambler picks and chooses his battles and understands he will lose some. The other extreme of this is being too afraid to take any risk and, yes, you will stay right on point with the curriculum (and may even finish early every week), but you won't get as much out of the program as you could. Intuitive, well-planned gambles can pay off big. Ignoring strong feelings toward taking a risk can blow great opportunities. Both are Shadows that The Gambler should avoid.

Recommendations

1. The Gambler takes educated risks. Know your participants, their issues, and their backgrounds before taking chances with them. This is gambling with people's feelings rather than with their money, but like with money you need to understand how much you can afford to lose. Keep that ratio in mind for the participants as well. Take only those risks that people seem ready to make movement toward. It's not smart gambling if you know you are pushing a father into a situation where he is not willing to change.

2. Be willing to take some risk. Some facilitators err on the side of caution to a fault. Every time you challenge a participant's belief system you are taking a gamble, but if you are not willing to challenge some of his beliefs he will never grow. People sign up for the group because they want more out of life. Participants are responsible for their own decisions. If you are in integrity and bring a challenge—a gamble—to a man and he rejects it, fine. Move on. You will not "win" every gamble in the sense that people will agree with your point of view, but you win by tactfully pointing out an issue that many people may be struggling with. And who knows, maybe you will win because you discover there is a better way to see the situation!

Power Question

You've heard some pessimists say, the only luck I have is bad luck. That's definitely not what this question is about. When luck is synonymous with good fortune, the Gambler asks:

Why are you feeling lucky?

12 The Strong Man

Affirmation

I am confident and powerful.

Description

The image of The Strong Man at the circus or a well buffed brother at the beach is a powerful one. It speaks to virility, discipline, and attractiveness. It exudes self-control and confidence. You will need some of these Strong Man's qualities to facilitate a successful fatherhood group. Physical strength is admirable, but being the physically strongest man in the room is not a necessity. Trust me on that. Being emotionally strong is helpful, but not so you can dominate other people. The most important place to display The Strong Man is in the relationship with your own fears. To be a successful facilitator, you must be confident you can get the job done.

The Strong Man facilitator demonstrates the confidence that comes with doing the work. Anyone can build big muscles by eating protein and lifting weights. Your message in the group is anyone can be a great father by participating in the group and practicing the activities at home. The Strong Man proves doing the group activities increases your self-worth. The Strong Man is confident that the program empowered him and he wants to the participants to experience that. The Strong Man figuratively carries the group on his wide shoulders. Whether you are physically muscular or skinny, every time you overcome a fear or limitation about facilitating, you are exercising The Strong Man. Participants will sense that power, be attracted to it, and will want to develop the same faith in their own actions.

Benefits of Discipline

As you discipline yourself into The Strong Man facilitator, you become more adept at digging into the subconscious without scorching yourself or others. The difference between our healthy instincts and our dangerous demons becomes more discernible as true power develops. How does this play out in a group? When you operate from a place of confidence with integrity, you weaken your desire to manipulate the men in the group, and others in your life, toward your own selfish ends.

The Strong Man is not interested in lording over other participants or his co-facilitator. The true Strong Man required to facilitate a group gains power over himself—self-mastery. You may not be able to bench press 300 pounds, but having the awareness and discipline to shut down the most charismatic guy in the group (even if it's you!) in order to draw out a comment from the quiet guy who looks like something is ruminating in his mind may require more intelligently targeted power.

The Strong Man is less concerned about aggrandizing himself and more genuinely interested in having each brother get the most out of the group. This may sound simple, but we all have experience with our ego manipulating us to get or do something that we know is out of harmony with our higher good. Though we know better, again and again we go unconscious and find the cookie stuffed in our mouth when we regain control of our senses. The Strong Man uses his strength, not so much, to keep the other participants in check; although that is a natural benefit. More importantly, The Strong Man keeps your other facilitator archetypes and shadows in check so you can successfully facilitate the group.

If you are not in touch with your deep, powerful core, you'll give off sketchy vibes in the group. Even if you are doing all the right things, they may not feel right to the men because the actions come from an inauthentic place within you. Facilitation is a journey of self-discovery and one thing you discover is power. If you are afraid to deal with your instincts, you are settling for being superficial and the group cannot succeed on a deep level with a superficial leader.

In our disconnected, pseudo-civilized culture we are cut off from our deeper selves. We may roar with false bravado pretending to reflect our deeper self, but our voice lacks depth. Inside we are frightened and confused. The more powerful thing is to admit our lack and by touching our true selves we activate a depth that is not present when pretending. Another way to think of this is you can't get strong, if you don't acknowledge where you are weak.

For example, confronting a disgruntled, angry participant head on may not be the right course. The true Strong Man may approach from another angle. Approaching the challenge with caution and compassion—neither angry nor fighting fire with fire—The Strong Man can calm the more boisterous adversary. I use this technique regularly in group. Men often come in roaring about a perceived, sometimes accurately (to me) sometimes not, offense. They do not want to hear another point of view, or hear you empathize with the other person (often the co-parent or child). They want to vent and be validated.

It's more powerful to approach this participant with your compassion and listen to his grievance even if you don't agree (sometimes people come to the group with very selfish notions) rather than disagreeing with what you hear him saying and immediately want to shut him down. You demonstrate The Strong Man by being magnanimous. You hear him out, and then you can offer other ideas, if he is opening to listening. You may have to role model listening many times for him before he is able to listen to you.

In a well run group participants look to your leadership. Some participants may be more comfortable staying in the role of follower. Your job as The Strong Man is not only to share your confidence with them, but help them cultivate the faith within themselves. Your goal is to develop the leader within them, not to let them always look to you (or any external source) for guidance. That is true strength.

Your tendency to entertain your lower self may not be fully eradicated as you become a better facilitator, but you become more aware of when it is on the rise. The Strong Man can afford to treat his adversaries with respect because he operates from a position of strength. Whether the adversary is alcoholism, womanizing, or gambling, treat your own lower self, and others', cautiously and respectfully as a skilled wild animal trainer would treat his subject. Our animal nature, like a wild animal, is not domesticated and, consequently, is dangerous. Gaining power over your lower, animal nature (for example, sloth, fear, disorganization, etc.) is how you acquire the power to facilitate groups.

Awareness is the first step in knowledge to develop The Strong Man. Too often we don't pay attention to our instinctive, animal side until it bursts from its cage and bites us in the ass. That's why repression is dangerous. You say you're not going to drink, look at porn, or buy a lotto. But you shove down your feelings, don't talk to friends, hide what's really going on and—*blam*—suddenly one night, you're watching porn on the computer, alternating between throwing back Hennessey and scratching lotto tickets, wishing you had more hands.

The Strong Man is disciplined. That's how he built those muscles, whether the muscles are physical, mental, emotional or spiritual. But the experienced Strong Man knows that breaks in discipline are necessary. You have to let the muscles rest to heal. You don't have to be strong all the time. Being vulnerable and unsure of yourself, the apparent opposite of The Strong Man, is how you learn new things.

Facilitator Example

I've emphasized the importance of exercising The Strong Man internally, and few places is this as vital as when you are reaching out to new participants. You see now that many of the other archetypes, like The Salesman, are powered by the strength of The Strong Man. You will have to overcome your reluctance to go out and make a fool of yourself. You may want to procrastinate. You may want to avoid it altogether, but as the leader unless you go out and do it, there will be no group.

I remember standing in the doorway of a preschool where I would be facilitating a group in a few weeks. Scores of parents walked by me in the 60 minutes I stood there during prime pick-up time, 5:00 to 6:00 pm. Almost everyone took the flyer I handed them. Few spoke more than a salutation. No one gave me contact information or the name of their child's father to follow up with him about attending the group.

Yet, I went back over the next two days and stood there for an hour recruiting fathers for the group. Part of me didn't want to return. I felt ignored and abandoned. However, The Strong Man remembered his discipline, overcame his fear of rejection and encouraged The Salesman to speak to every person who walked by.

The second day, I got a couple of names and phone numbers to follow up with. My confidence grew. The third day was even better. Like always, I found my 13 guys to start the group; the majority finished and loved it. Amid their thank you's to me during graduation, I knew we were all there because I developed The Strong Man to speak up for what I believed in and convinced other people to attend the group. The Salesman may do the talking, but The Strong Man makes sure he is in the right place at the right time.

Participant Example

Every man walks into the father's group circle demonstrating his strength. He certainly doesn't get support from mainstream masculine culture to join a fathers' group and talk about his relationships. Participants are told in so many ways that real men—traditionally Strong Men—are out hunting, working, sexing or watching football. This desire to work on our inner life is not consistent with traditional masculinity. So to break away from this false ideology is itself a show of strength, power, and independent thought. This was exhibited by a friend of my young daughter who got nabbed by me on the phone simply because our daughters were friends. I met Tony once at a school event. I had seen his fiancée at the school many times and only talked to him briefly on that one occasion, but it was enough to give me the courage to call him out.

It took him a little while to commit after I initially called and I made regular check-in calls before and during the first few weeks of the group. Eventually, he became very animated in the sessions and shared stories about how growing up without a father in his life had made him anxious about how to interact with his daughter. It took a tremendous amount of strength for him to be vulnerable with us in the group. He was able to reflect on his fear of connecting with his daughter which had actually resulted in his doing the exact thing he was afraid of. Tony began building on the time he spent with his daughter and not being so afraid that he might do something wrong. By admitting a fear that he'd never acknowledged before, Tony was able to address it and propel his behavior toward the goals he held for himself.

He explained all this himself at the graduation, when he spoke in front of his peers from the group, his fiancée and his daughter:

> "When I was invited to this group, I thought, *What good is gonna come from a bunch of guys sitting around talking?* But a lot of good came out of it. I became a better dad and got a lot of new friends. I never knew what real brotherhood felt like before. I love you guys."

Tony may not have added inches to his chest and biceps but that sounds like real strength to me.

Shadow

When you begin to facilitate groups, you will have to deal with a tendency to misuse your strength. You acquire power when you lead a group. How you use the power you generate will determine how successful you become as a facilitator. People will participate in the groups you facilitate because they sense of an environment of safety and growth. Despite being betrayed by friends in the past and hearing regular stories in the news about people being taken advantage of by someone they trusted, the participants trust you.

As leader of a fathers' group you may not be inclined to exploit money or sexual favors (two frequently exploited objects) from group members, but there are other areas where The Strong Man might misuse his power. One is simply being a hypocrite, not being a nurturing father yourself. You aren't expected to be a paragon of perfect parenting 24/7. You will lose your temper and make parenting mistakes. There are times when your best parenting move will be to role model repentance. Group participants observe your stories closely. You are a role model for them. Owning that is important. Unless you've become infallible, The Strong Man will, at times, misuse some of the power he generates. Don't beat up on yourself too hard, but learn from your mistakes. One reason you facilitate groups is to learn how to generate and be trusted with greater amounts of power *so you can do more good.*

To get to this level of authority, you must have disciplined yourself enough to recruit men, study the program principles and tame dangerous tendencies. That's what the lower nature represents . . . our dangerous tendencies. Maybe in the group you want to take advantage of your power by subtly making fun of someone in the group, or worse, someone who's not in the group. You may think it's all in good fun, but it's a misuse of power. The Strong Man is so glamorous in masculine culture, admired by men and women alike that it's tempting to overdo it. But, it is possible to harm the body by becoming too strong, using chemical enhancements that actually weaken and destroy the body in the long run. In an emotional sense, it's also possible to overdo your power.

Emotional bullying is an example of this and it's a keynote of weak facilitation. It's easy to use the intimacy developed in the group as fodder to manipulate people into disclosing information that they'd rather not and then using that information to belittle and shame them:

> "Oh, remember when you told us Dolores was angry with you for not having a job now, maybe that's why she's cheating on you. You got to man up, bro."

Another limitation that can develop in The Strong Man, of both the physical and emotional variety, is a lack of flexibility. This is a result of The Strong Man becoming over-controlling. Flexibility and vulnerability are complementary skills for The Strong Man. The Strong Man can become so rigid in any of his disciplines that he could rush past an epiphany that would have been a major insight for every participant in the group. Don't do this.

The overarching danger in using The Strong Man is getting too caught up in the glory of power and not being aware of when to shift to another perspective. Remember, there are 21 other archetypes and they are all necessary.

Recommendations

1. Temper The Strong Man with love. Resist the inner tendency and societal encouragement to bully others who have less power than you. Let The Strong Man be guided by The Mystic, The Mother Hen and other archetypes. Use The Strong Man to support the participants in your group who are just finding their voice. The school yard analogy is to use your strength to help defend the weaker members of the community.

2. Don't be afraid to show The Strong Man, both with yourself and other people. In the effort to humanize men, there are some unmanly messages being given to men that not only circumscribe over-the-top aggressiveness, but also undermine useful contributions The Strong Man makes to society. Don't be afraid to stake a claim, make a judgment, or call a spade a spade. The men in your group may not always agree with it, but if it's done respectfully, you will both learn from it.

Power Question

The Strong Man asks:

Why are you confident and powerful?

13 The Diplomat

Affirmation

I connect what appears conflicted.

Description

The Diplomat is an erudite fellow and consummate communicator. He is a peacemaker and a man about town. He employs old world charm and street corner smarts. He is precise in his thinking and language and doesn't stoop to saying something simply to score brownie points. For these reasons, people enjoy his company. His "super-vision" allows him to see what others may be too short-sighted to observe without his facile intervention. The Diplomat doesn't dictate; he guides so gently, others are happy to move in the direction suggested because they see their own self-interest along that path.

One becomes The Diplomat through recognizing we are all connected at some level and then exposing that connection when two or more parties are reveling in conflict. The Diplomat wants us to bury the hatchet in a safe place so there is less conflict in the circle, community and planet. He sees a way that swords can be beaten into plowshares. As a fathers' group facilitator, The Diplomat is courageous enough to reach out to misunderstood and misunderstanding group participants, men who are polarized, who are angry, and who have calcified ideas into things they believe are real.

The key component of these miscommunications is that participants firmly believe in their own ways of thinking and behaving. But The Diplomat has a sophisticated level of awareness and recognizes that the beliefs which disconnect and cause disagreement are only a couple of the infinite ways participants can choose to look at a situation. You may be called to activate The Diplomat when two or more participants in your group are interacting in a conflicting manner. Or you may need to exercise The Diplomat to help resolve a conflict between a participant and a family member who is not in your group. The Diplomat can uplift either situation as long as initially, at least, one person in the conflict can expand his thinking to consider other connections and consequences that were not evident before. When one person shifts his beliefs about the conflict, often the other party responds in kind.

The Diplomat is much more than a referee, but acting like a referee may play into the early stage of The Diplomat's work. When the connection between two people is contentious, it is important to pause momentarily. That is one responsibility a referee has—blowing the whistle to stop a play in progress to draw attention to an infraction. After issuing a judgment, a referee then simply allows the conflicting parties to reengage at the same level of awareness. The Diplomat's pause, however, is followed by the addition of an idea or two—not necessarily a judgment, which is another contrast with a referee—which allows the parties to reengage at a higher level of awareness. In this way, The Diplomat acts as a mediator for the conflict.

The classic case involves a father expressing frustration over a disagreement with the mother of his child. The Diplomat and other group members can hold the position for the opposing viewpoint, which may vex the participant. Then The Diplomat exposes and connects a truth that exists in each position. Let's say you have a participant who is upset because he works a couple of jobs to support the family while the mother of his children stays home and he feels she doesn't keep the house clean. The cleanliness of the house becomes something they argue about constantly. He complains about it every week during the group.

After establishing a pause in the action, The Diplomat looks for commonalities in the two perspectives and finds a link between them. "Are the children well taken care of?" he may ask the participant. The father reports he has no complaints about how the mom takes care of the kids, but the house is a mess! Well, now, you've got a point of connection which The Diplomat points out: both Mom and Dad want the children to be well clothed, fed and clean, and that seems to be happening. This begins the experience of diplomacy, and while it might be a satisfying end point for the mother—if she were present—it feels unsatisfying and inconclusive to the father in the group. That's because it's not over. The Diplomat doesn't look for one-sided compromises. Not so much because that wouldn't be fair; fairness is relative—what's fair to one, may not be fair to another. The Diplomat doesn't promote one-sided compromises because they *do not join what is separate*.

So he asks the father, "With all the mess in the house, is there one area that you want to be organized more than any other?" The dad senses where The Diplomat is going and doesn't want to give in so easily.

He replies, "I want the whole house cleaned like it should be."

One of the keys about The Diplomat is that he is able to maintain an optimistic perspective as he hunts for the connections he knows exist. He helps participants and their family members remember their fundamental bond while exploring their ideas that happen to conflict. It may take the father in the above scenario some time to accept the proposal that he and the mother of his children cleaning one area of the house initially has a higher probability of success than constantly arguing about the condition of the whole house. Even without the other party being present when one person in a conflict begins to operate from a higher level of awareness, the entire problem shifts. That's the power of The Diplomat facilitating a fathers' group.

Facilitator Example

There are many situations when you will be called on to be The Diplomat. Often it occurs when one of the participants is working through a challenging situation with the mother of his children and you provide diplomacy with her in absentia. The Diplomat must make a connection with both parties in the dispute and when one is not present you have to be even more careful to establish the opposing point of view. That way when the participant reenacts or describes the diplomacy process in the group with his partner who was absent she will feel the integrity of the process and feel a sense of buy-in.

There will be times when group members disagree on a topic being discussed to the point where The Diplomat must jump in and help sort through contentious feelings, but those are easier to manage because both parties are in the room. One of the biggest honors as The Diplomat may be to be asked to personally mediate a dispute in the home of a participant. This can be volatile territory and you can always choose to refer the couple or family to a therapist if you don't feel up to the challenge. If you accept the call, you must remember the rule of looking for truth and connection on both sides of the argument. Emotionally or physically abusive situations need correction before this can be applied.

In the curriculum I used most frequently, there's one week when all the dads are asked to bring their children for father-child games and play. Larry had a 10-month old daughter who, he told us, his wife did not want him to bring.

He looked sullen as he told us, "She says I don't spend enough time with Angela. I asked if she wanted to come with us, but she said she'd feel uncomfortable around a group of dads."

This seemed like an easy lift for The Diplomat. I wasn't even aiming to get Larry's wife to let him bring Angela alone if she didn't think he spent enough time with her to handle that, even though I thought he was up to the task from how he described his role as a dad. I just wanted to reassure her that she would be comfortable at the group. It wasn't as easy as I thought. Larry gave me permission to call and she wasn't shy about sharing her point of view.

"I don't know what Larry tells you all in there, but he hardly ever spends any time with Angela," she started.

I assured her Larry wasn't telling us he was a 24/7 dad. It took about 20 minutes to persuade her that the fathers' playgroup would be a welcoming place for her and Angela. In the end, all three of them ended up having a great time. They got a lot of praise from the other dads for being a beautiful family and I believe it was a turning point for how Larry's wife thought of him as a father. At the graduation, the mom told me she would have trusted Larry to bring Angela alone to the celebration – except she wanted to come back and be a part of good times!

Participant Example

A well run fathers' group brings out the best in men, and inspiring The Diplomat within the participants is a good example. You will probably notice many of your group participants demonstrating qualities of The Diplomat during group; you also might hear them report examples of using The Diplomat in their homes. One of my favorites is an older dad named Ray who was having problems with his teenage daughter. It seemed he, his wife and their daughter were constantly arguing about the girl's curfew, cell phone usage and time spent on the computer. Their daughter got mostly A's in school and she felt like she should have more privileges at home. Ray and his wife wanted to keep a tight rein on her and her younger siblings and as immigrants, were worried about what they saw as the lenient aspects of American culture.

Throughout the course of our fathers' group, Ray started listening to his 15-year-old daughter's case more closely and decided she had some valid points. His next step was to speak with his wife privately about his new perspective on the situation. His wife was initially as dead set against granting more privileges as he had been. But over a period of a few weeks, Ray nonchalantly "held talks" with the mom that focused on gradually relaxing the restrictions on their eldest, provided she continued to do well in school and complete her chores at home. Mom agreed to a few small compromises in their rules that made their daughter happy not only because she got to stay out a little later, and use the computer and talk on the phone more, but also because she felt like her parents were listening to her as she got older. Last I heard she was still on the honor roll.

Shadow

Neville Chamberlain is the most ignoble diplomat of modern times. He was the British Prime Minister before and at the beginning of

World War II. He has the unfortunate legacy of being duped by Adolph Hitler into signing a series of negotiated agreements which were intended to prevent the war from escalating. Basically, Chamberlain compromised too much and this is the deepest shadow element of The Diplomat. In an effort to avoid conflict, The Diplomat may fail to stand up for what's right and end up neither avoiding conflict nor keeping his integrity intact. The Diplomat works to resolve conflict while understanding that sometimes people will be unreasonable and need to be confronted about their unreasonableness. Unfortunately, sometimes this results in arguments, fights and war.

A close second for demonstrating The Diplomat's shadow in the 20th century was one of the United States' most famous victims of police brutality, Rodney King. Following the acquittal in 1992 of four Los Angeles police officers who were unknowingly filmed beating and kicking King as they arrested him for speeding and evading arrest, riots erupted in Los Angeles and several other cities, killing 53 and injuring thousands. During the conflicts, King made an infamous appearance on television designed to quell the riots in which he pleaded, "Can we all get along?"

The phrase immediately became fodder for social commentators and comedians as an example of insincere diplomacy. Because the police officers' acquittal was seen by many as a blatant miscarriage of justice, parading the victim of the initial injustice on television was seen as a manipulative act by power brokers in Los Angeles that showed no regard for real compromise or joining together.

A willingness to engage in confrontation is a necessary element of success for The Diplomat. Working to avoid conflict at any cost is not a true sign of The Diplomat who underneath his sophistication has a very courageous character. If there is a conflict within your fathers' group or that group members have within their families, The Diplomat engages participants in a process that joins the opposing ideas and seeks mutual benefit. But if that is not working, at some point a good facilitator shifts to another archetype.

Recommendations

1. Be on the lookout for simpatico elements of all disagreements. You can almost always find common elements in any conflict if you remain calm, creative and look for them. One of the biggest causes of missing these similarities is being focused on the intense frustration of the parties you're working with. Their frustration rubs off on you and you become agitated, unable to find the links that could connect people. Whenever you find yourself talking to a participant who is angry at what another person did, take a breath and calm yourself. Practice doing this until you can join with that participant while at the same time feeling expansive enough to see any rationale in the other person's point of view.

2. If you really don't see a rationale in the other person's point of view, don't be afraid to say it. The Diplomat needs to be an honest man to be trusted by both sides. If you continually find truth where there is only murkiness and shadows, your credibility as one who can unite around commonality will rightfully be questioned. Sometimes you will be called to say that it seems one of the positions in the disagreement is based on erroneous information or beliefs. That's the best you can do.

Power Question

The Diplomat *sees* things in a different way than non-diplomatic, inclined-to-aggress people. It's not enough to know how he does it. In addition, ponder:

Why does The Diplomat connect what appears conflicted?

14 The Closer

Affirmation

It's safe for me to complete.

Description

To be an excellent facilitator, you need to exercise The Closer. You need to skillfully end a participant's rambling monologue. You need to conscientiously close group sessions on time. You need to graciously lead the group series to completion. To facilitate well, you need to be able to terminate well.

The Salesman is great at recruiting participants by discovering their needs and aligning them with the benefits which are achievable in the group. But even The Salesman won't be a success if he doesn't know how to close the deal. That means in addition to sharing the benefits, The Salesman has to ask potential recruits to attend. Many Salesmen are afraid to close. They feel like if they never clearly ask a potential recruit to attend, they'll never be rejected. That may be true but they'll also lose most of their "sales."

Closing involves taking a stand, whether it's asking a customer if he wants to buy that car or asking William who's been rambling in your group about nothing important for five minutes to hold that thought so you can move on. You've got to have confidence to close. But whether you're selling cars or facilitating groups, you can't be an asshole when you close or you'll lose the sale. You've got to empathize with the person you are putting on the spot.

Sometimes you put more than one guy on the spot. A good facilitator inspires participants so much that some will want to keep the conversation going beyond the official closing time. A great facilitator closes the group anyway. Even though the conversation is juicy and people feel connected, it's important to remember other things are going on outside. When the group is in the zone being there seems more important than whatever the dads had planned to do after the group. Not one dad is making a move to leave. You're tempted to squeeze the vibe and let the group run a few minutes late. What harm could come of it? In fact, a few of the guys showed up late, so you'd only be taking back what you lost in the beginning due to their tardiness.

Don't do it! Even if you start late you must end the group on time to set a good example and respect the men's time. People who feel excited to spend a few extra minutes in the group talking about behavior change in a two-year-old child or a 30-year-old spouse will come to regret the consequences. They'll feel pissed when they missed that child's bedtime, or it's too late to stop at the store after group like they planned, then they get home and walk into a conflict with that 30-year-old spouse. They'll throw you and the group under the bus in a minute and their attendance next week will be in jeopardy. Close late consistently and you will lose group members.

The fathers in your group may just be realizing how much they really enjoy the weekly communion and how important it's become to them, when the truth that this is a finite experience which will be over sooner than they wish hits them. At the end of every fathers' group I've ever facilitated, most of the participants want to stay and do more. And the same is true for every well run group I've heard of. The group space fills a deep yearning in men that most of us didn't even know we had. Because of the limitations of funding and capacity, you may not have the luxury to keep going with a single group of men. If you're doing this as part of a grant funded project, you probably have to get new fathers every time, you may not have the luxury of working with one group of worthy individuals forever.

Benefits of Completion

Since you're going to have to end each group, you need to learn to terminate well. As it's written, all things have a season, and completing a group well is one of the most important steps in facilitation. A good curriculum will have useful completion activities which may include giving the men a chance to say goodbye to each other in the group and state things they like, respect, or have seen change about other dads. But just like high school, college, and other courses of study, helping people move on well includes, in part, helping them connect to beneficial programs or activities that can take them to the next level. Knowing what's available to refer dads to in your community is helpful in terminating.

You can't cheat The Closer because not only is this archetype essential at the end of a series, he's essential during every single group session. One of the most important skills that a great facilitator needs is to know how to stop people from talking without them feeling devalued. People love to talk about themselves and a large part of most fathering curricula operate right in that sweet spot. Part of your goal is getting participants to self-reflect and then share those insights with others. To most of the men in the group who have not had the experience of having their deep thoughts and feelings valued, this experience can be like finding gold coins in an old, dark basement. Even the initially quiet group members will discover they love it and want more.

At first your job is to open the participants up, then your job becomes shutting them down. All the men will have had lots of experience of being shut down inconsiderately: as children; on the job; with their partners. As facilitator, you must learn to terminate their insights and shared reflections with compassion and consideration, in a way that leaves them feeling open to share another time. This can seem tricky at first, but is definitely something you can learn to do with aplomb. The trick is to empathize with the speaker.

There are times when people are sharing something deep and significant and deserve a little more time than usual, but this is not frequent. More often, group participants have plenty of time to get to their point in the first few minutes of their floor time and by the time you have to step in and terminate their roll, they have slipped into what is politely called palaver, but more accurately described as hot air. They are just filling up aural space because you gave them the opportunity. Participants will often feel grateful for you stepping in to terminate their monologue because they knew it was going nowhere.

Still, you need to do it with finesse. I've found hand gestures are a great way to start. If you start with your voice you will have to speak over the speaker and even if he is out in verbal nowhere land this can appear rude or even hostile. Gently holding up your hand, at chest height, with your elbow deeply bent in the universal gesture of stop should be enough to get his and the group's attention. You may have to do this a few seconds until the speaker's current burst of steam runs out. If this doesn't get your speaker to stop, leaning a little forward in you chair with both hands held out is a stronger gesture to use before adding your voice.

In a group based on love and compassion, it's a good idea to avoid the harsher gestures of termination, like hands forming a capitol "T" as in time-out, and certainly the extreme finger across the throat as in "cut" is not appropriate in a friendly interaction. If the speaker doesn't get the message with one or two hands held up, it will be necessary to use your voice. You are the facilitator and by now the other men in the group are: one, probably all also bored with Brother Talk-Too-Much and, two, aware that he's ignoring your direction and curious how this tiny bit of tension will play out.

When you start speaking, it's always safe to apologize for interrupting and refer back to the ground rules or group norms which should include something about sharing air space. When you interrupt, another qualifier is to give the dad 20 or 30 seconds to wrap things up. Don't be overgenerous at this point; a minute is too long. Then when you go to full shutdown mode everyone is expecting it. Although it may feel awkward to interrupt the flow and move on you will have to. If you don't limit the talkers in your group, you will have no group. This is essential. Everyone in the group understands this dynamic and will consider you a failed leader if you don't make the move when a talker is monopolizing air space. Do it in a nice way, but do it.

Terminating a session is a little less harrowing because it's not one specific father you need to interrupt, but the act still requires resolve because you could have the momentum of the entire group pushing for a few minutes more. Or, you may get so caught up in the moment that you lose track of time—not good for a facilitator.

Even if you have to haphazardly eliminate a wonderful exercise you were planning to do, skip it if you will go over. If participants are fired up about a discussion the group is enjoying as you approach end time, try and take a couple of minutes to cool it down before you conclude the session. Let a few voices reflect on the discussion you were having, do your best to sum it yourself, give them a charge to think about the discussion over the week and then let them go. If one or two individuals seemed like they had a hard time digesting some of the ideas generated in the circle, plan to talk to them as individuals either after class, if it seems urgent, or give them a call the next day. Participants will start next week's group in better spirits and more timely if they know they are leaving at the time you promised.

As far as terminating the final sessions in a series, some participants prefer to ignore the end of a group cycle. It's the same sort of denial that makes people not want to think about dying. Many men feel uncomfortable talking about how we will miss one another after we transition. Some participants act like the end of the group is no big deal; others skip the final sessions to try and shortcut the inevitable. The best, most honest way to deal with the end of a cycle is to talk about it early as a natural part of group life. I often tell people in the first group session that they will become attached to one another and sad when we have to end. Most participants are incredulous at this statement. They can't believe they'll actually miss these strangers.

In order to get that big bang at the end though, you have to keep people living in the present. That old idea, "If you're afraid of death, you're afraid of life" resonates with groups, too. If you are too much looking forward to or too much resisting the end of the group, you'll have a hard time being in the present. The insight and joy that the fathers get from doing each session activity is what makes them reminisce fondly about what they will no longer have. As you start to prepare participants in the last half of the group for the ending, it's good to remind people that nothing in nature is ever lost. The changes in attitude and behavior that are inspired in the group can be carried on forever, as the feeling of affection in our hearts for the group will be.

In fact, by completing the group, dads become part of a special cohort of men around the planet who carry shared positive memories of male group activity. Sport teams, fraternities, and soldiers all have a sense of this, although the activities that bond vary greatly, of course. Maybe we'll even reach a "100th Monkey" scenario when a critical mass of men have adopted a nurturing father's mentality and all men will automatically start to act in a more nurturing manner. We know there's strength in numbers, so even without reunion meetings after their group graduates, dads who have had the experience can still be light bearers for men still in the shadows of abusive or neglectful behavior toward their families.

Still, the difficult problem of saying goodbye exists. You should acknowledge it openly, starting around the midpoint of the program and more frequently in the last few weeks. Check in with individual men about how their experience in the group has been and what kinds of connection they would like with other men after the group ends. Many men look at support as a dirty word. We're supposed to support ourselves! We give support, we don't take it. That's why it's important to gradually reframe the group as a way to connect with other men. We are all social creatures and, as men, we already have some connection with other men. But what kind is it? And what kind do we want?

Each participant must ask himself, "Does the connection/support I currently receive from other men (and women) in my life encourage me in becoming the individual I intend to be? If not, how can I create more positive connections after the group has terminated?

During the group, participants discover how powerful it is to simply speak with and listen to others. Men learn how important it is to have other people acknowledge what's going on in our lives. We get why our girlfriends are always jumping on the phone with one another and why psychotherapy is a multi-billion dollar industry.

Talking helps. Listening helps. Whom will you talk to and listen to when the group is over? Relying solely on your partner to satisfy this deep need to communicate and be understood may not be sufficient. Maybe you two have too much baggage together. The male peer support group is a fantastic idea because we understand each other as men, but we're not as invested in the outcomes of each other's actions as our co-parents are. Part of your termination strategy should be helping the men in the group set up a formal (counseling, church) or informal (group of friends) network of emotional support for themselves. It's like putting on your oxygen mask first in an airplane crisis. If the guys in your group cannot take care of themselves, they will not be able to take care of anyone else. Getting commitments from them on this point is one of the best things you can do for the men in your group—and their families.

Another important benefit of The Closer is the opportunity to celebrate life. Usually for a physical death we wait until the person is gone to say what a great person he was, and how much we will miss him. In the group, we do this in a more proactive way by acknowledging each dad while he is alive and in the group. There's an appreciation activity that's done at the conclusion of many curricula I've seen. I encourage you to use something similar. During the last session, each man has the light of love shined on him and every member of the group says something they liked, respected, or saw change in him. This is one of the most memorable and moving parts of the program. Men who wouldn't give each other the time of day three months ago now share sincere, heartfelt accolades for one another.

In current kindergarten culture, kids might be discouraged from participating in an activity where one member is singled out for more praise than another. But in the authentic culture that develops in the fathers' groups we all know which member will get the most praise. I also know the brothers become too connected to leave any man out in the cold. Truth and Compassion have become hallmarks of our interactions. And truly any man who stuck through all those conversations is so understood by his peers that they can't help but find something good to say about him. As facilitator, you should also make sure you receive a round of honest appreciation; you have the opportunity to model healthy self-esteem without allowing your ego to be blown up to where you monopolize the activity. Mainly, let the light shine on all the participant heroes. That will leave a better impression in people's minds.

I welcome enthusiastic participants to repeat the program, but don't allow the possibility of their reappearance to keep you from working hard to recruit new members. If a highly motivated father wants to participate in another group and you have space—fine. But don't allow the recycling of graduates, who've already experienced the magic of a group, prevent you from being diligent about going out and recruiting new participants.

Facilitator Example

Bob is an alpha male. Six feet and change, handsome, dynamic and smart, he's a person who draws attention when he walks in a room. People seem to enjoy (or at least tolerate) listening to him without interruption. When I'm not in facilitator mode, I enjoy it as well. Although I love an audience too, I don't have the need to be the center of attention as much as it appears Bob does. Normally, I would not interrupt him, but when he's in my group I do.

Bob has lots of theories for why men and women act the way they do and he often peppers them with reflections on his own experiences. When it was Bob's turn to discuss how parenting tasks were divided in his home after breaking down the shared responsibilities briefly, he launched into a sociological treatise about the legacy of primal man in modern life. The other men in the group nodded in agreement. Bob had thought this out more than they had and he started taking them to school. The problem was, this wasn't school. It was my fathering *group*.

I held up my hand when sitting forward in my chair didn't catch his attention. "Excuse me, Bob," I interrupted his monologue. "What you are saying makes a lot of sense. Unfortunately if we spend more time on it now, we won't be able to get to everyone's story tonight and I really need to make that happen."

"Oh, sure, of course, no problem," Bob replied amiably.

He was happy to stop. He *knew* he was on borrowed time and was happy to stand down once I figuratively stood up, but he wouldn't have done it on his own. There are lots of Bobs in the world and if you are not comfortable or at least willing to interrupt them, they will take over your group. Don't let that happen.

Participant Example

The Closer archetype, whether he appears during a participant monologue, at the scheduled end of a session, or at the completion of an entire series, represents good boundaries. Empathy is a necessary skill for relationships, but in the quest to develop the ability to connect, some may ignore the ability to cut off. Participants sometimes display this dysfunction. There was a dad named Dennis in one of my groups who was having awful problems with the mother of his daughter. Granted, I only heard one side of the story, but from his consistent descriptions she was abusive, manipulative, angry and just plain old mean much of the time. Police were regularly called to the home and his feeling of safety was compromised.

He and the other men discussed many ways to improve his situation over the weeks and finally someone suggested that he officially move out. He was already staying with other family members about half the week because of various conflicts in his home. The idea of terminating the live-in part of their relationship resonated with him. It removed the power of his partner cutting him off willy-nilly and contrary to his initial fears moving out actually provided more stability for his daughter. Everything has a season and not recognizing the end of a season shows a lack of awareness. Dennis discovered that by manifesting The Closer, he was able to be more fully present and a new chapter opened up with his daughter and her mom.

Shadow

There is a continuum of closing. In the murky shadows at one end of the continuum you find yourself closing too hard, too fast and with little feeling. On the other end is undisciplined, overly loose facilitation that allows every rambling monologue to take over the group. Neither is good. The participants want and need structure for the group and that is impossible to provide without having a strong grasp of closing strategies.

Fear and inappropriate social cues will lead you down the wrong path of facilitation. You *know* when a dad in your group has gone on too long. Not only is there the objective time limit you provide for each participant, there is an inner knowing that the dad is grandstanding or filibustering or simply rambling. If you fail to interrupt and close at that point, you need to do some soul searching regarding the messages you accepted about social interactions and hierarchy. Closing down anyone adroitly takes skill. Closing down a man who might intimidate you in other circumstances takes skill and fortitude. If you cannot build the confidence to interrupt people in your group who you feel have more power than you in other areas (size, money, position, charisma, etc.), you will never become a master facilitator. It's that simple.

On the other hand, if your own sense of privilege and entitlement is so strong that you feel free to shut down everyone else in the group because you know you can explain a point, illustrate a story, and amuse the participants better than this schmuck who is holding the floor, you're too full of yourself and will not take a group of men to its full potential. You must be the ringmaster, but nobody wants to see the ringmaster when the trapeze artists are doing their thing. You have to find a balance and create space for everyone in the group to share. That's one powerful difference between a group and a class.

Recommendations

1. Give people a warning. Foreshadow the end of each session before you get there so dads aren't surprised if they lost track of time. Give dads 20 or 30 seconds to wrap up their comments before you cut them off. Get people ready for the end of a group cycle by talking about it for a few weeks before it happens, and check in with participants about their plans for staying connected with positive, uplifting men (and women) when the group concludes.

2. Acknowledge the importance of closing – for everything there is a season. To help a dad feel listened to and valued, sum up the theme of his comments when you stop him for going on too long. Honor your group by creating a celebration at the end of your group cycle. Completing a fathers' group is an accomplishment. Achieving this level of connection and intimacy is not encouraged in our culture, especially for men. This is behavior to be proud of. Make sure you recognize it with the guys at the end.

Power Question

Terminating well is a skill. That's why football teams practice a two-minute drill and coaches specially designate baseball pitchers to end an inning or game. Beginnings require closings. Ask yourself: How am I a good closer?

15 The Artist

Affirmation

I create enlightening experiences.

Description

The Artist creates a thing out of an idea. That's what you do with every group, with every session. Even though you may be using a curriculum that another Artist created, you can bet the fathers' curriculum you are using did not exist in that form 30 or 40 years ago. Who had the idea? Where did it come from? Just like the old paint by numbers paintings, you are piggybacking on The Artist who created the curriculum. But you have to use your own creativity to implement the curriculum and each application of it will be different based on the way you see and experience life. Just as importantly, the group that you are facilitating would exist unless *you* created it.

Where did your inspiration come from? Where did your resolve to fulfill the inspiration come from? They both came from your thoughts. Then you used your willpower to build something beautiful that had never existed before. The Artist is a crucial facilitator archetype. No group gets off the ground without The Artist. The Artist takes a flash of intuition and follows it through to fruition. The Artist must by nature be a contrarian. He must be comfortable turning the status quo upside down. Modern Western culture does not honor The Artist or inventor while they are producing their Art.

Instead, well-meaning people living in their mental boxes tell you it cannot or should not be done, that your idea is impractical or unattractive. No matter how miserable people are, most are afraid of change. They don't want you to rock the boat even if it's sinking and there's an island close by! Facilitating a fathers' group is inherently creative and "Don't be creative" is a message many of us have gotten since childhood. It's reflected in how our society thinks of The Artist (and I'm not referring to Prince during his dispute with Warner Brothers). The Artist is seen as an unstable person who starves. Who wants to embrace that? In her 1992 book *The Artist's Way*, Julia Cameron talks about the blocked creative that is inside of all of us. That's the side that you need to let free to build your groups.

Benefits of Creative Power

The Artist does derive his ideas somewhat mysteriously, and all successful artists have the discipline to follow through on their flashes of insight and intuition. Want to write a book, star in a play, run a dads' group? These are all great ideas that many people harbor inside, but the more "practical," grown-up part of your personality may say, "Don't be silly. You can't do that." Well, you can. You must! All of us came to Earth with a mission and if you feel called to run groups, you'll probably feel frustrated and let down until you step up and make it happen. That takes real courage.

So The Artist plays a strong role in getting the group under way, but your flashes of creative intuition don't stop once the group gets started. In fact, you should use the wealth of awareness available to The Artist to improve your group at every decision point along the way. Any curriculum you use will only take you so far. You are going to have to implement the group yourself with unforeseen occurrences and challenges that will have to be dealt with on the fly. Your connection to your creative power will largely determine how well those situations are managed.

Facilitator Example

This is a favorite example of mine. I was facilitating a group in a room right off a busy urban street. The fathers had been meeting for about two months and had a nice connection going. There was an apartment house across the street from where we met that often had a lot of people hanging in front—loud alcohol fueled music and talk, you know the deal. Well, this one summer evening as we were having a deep, healing discussion about how we had been hurt and what we had learned from relationships we've been in, we heard an argument escalating between two women outside.

It wasn't clear from what we heard if the conflict was over money or a man or something else, but it was pretty clear from the voices that these two women could come to blows any second. From the sound of the argument and our knowledge of the street, it was clear that several other people were involved, as instigators or bystanders, waiting for something to jump off. Of course, I considered walking the group out there to help level the vibe. But I knew the appearance of eight unknown men who were not government anointed peace keepers would initially escalate the conflict.

The entire rest of our session would be taken up with this unplanned and unsolicited intervention. Didn't seem like a good idea.

After a few more shouted verbal taunts back and forth across the street, an idea flashed in my mind. I acknowledged the conflict and asked everyone to send concentrated healing vibes to the women and their friends who were involved. We took about a minute to silently visualize a peaceful conclusion to the volatile situation. Like a miracle, the arguing immediately quieted as we concentrated our healing thoughts on the porch across the street. All the men in the group, including me, were awed by the transformation. We finished our discussion with no other verbal explosions outside. It was an amazing piece of public art that I had not planned, but was delighted that the intuition flashed into my head and that I had the courage to execute it. That's the power of The Artist!

Participant Example

By creating something that didn't exist before, The Artist breaks the status quo in terms of rules they were given in their roles as dads. You can consider the result a good outcome or you may consider the result a bad outcome. That's the thing about art: not everyone likes what The Artist creates.

But dads will take the opportunity of joining your group to think creatively and problem solve parenting challenges that were previously intractable. Nelson was one dad who came to the group with a 'tween son who was having serious emotional problems at home and school. He didn't have friends in school. He didn't get along with his older brother and younger sister at home. He seemed miserable and seemed to enjoy making everyone around him miserable too.

Nelson was excited to come to the group and was one of very few participants who initiated contact with me. He called me after his wife saw a flyer posted at a neighborhood health center. He talked about his middle child, Richard, a lot during the group and he tried several interventions at home that we discussed in the group like: listening to his son's feelings more; making sure he and his wife were consistent with discipline; talking to the school staff to make sure Richard wasn't feeling bullied in school. On a follow up call between sessions, I mentioned the possibility of Richard seeing a psychotherapist. Nelson had a pretty strong negative reaction, so I tried to normalize it and backed off some. Although Richard sounded depressed, I hadn't heard that he sounded suicidal and Nelson was having a hard time with the idea of therapy. I would have pushed harder if it sounded like Richard was in imminent danger of some sort.

A couple of weeks after this discussion, one of the men in the group asked if Nelson had thought about counseling for Richard and describe his own positive response to talking to a therapist.

Nelson said, "Yeah, Haji mentioned that too and I've been thinking about it."

Before the group ended Nelson and his wife started taking Richard to meet with a psychotherapist. Nelson reported in the group that he felt a lot less tension in the home because – even if Richard's behavior had not changed dramatically yet – all the family members felt like *something* was happening and better outcomes were in store. A solution the family could not have envisioned a few months before was making a positive difference in their lives. The Artist participant had broken the mold and created something good in the family that had not existed before.

Shadow

We are all familiar with The Artist's Shadow. His outsized personality and influence on the culture has assured that his shadow casts a strong impression in our collective imagination. In brief, The Artist Shadow is unreliable. Most people already think of The Artist as unstable, immature, a diva and, let's not forget, starving. Art is not seen as a "normal" profession. Ultimately, The Artist is seen as selfish, someone who must follow his vision at the cost of all else, not the sort of bloke you want managing other people.

While there may be some truth in the negative, stereotypical characteristics associated with The Artist, these can be sublimated by holding to the vision of what being a creative person in the service of a well facilitated group means. Because The Artist naturally breaks from the status quo of what is expected of a good corporate (academic, military, non-profit, etc.) soldier, he is bound to create some angst among the cube dwellers. By focusing on the highest creative expression of the fathers' group, you are less likely to ruffle feathers unnecessarily.

Because The Artist is, in large part, an inward-looking archetype, like The Mystic, the potential to distort messages received internally is a definite possibility. It can be helpful for The Artist to have a trusted colleague that he can bounce ideas off before springing them on the group. Sometimes that's not possible because of timing, so it may be necessary to use the group as a sounding board for your artistic innovations. People will appreciate your unorthodox ideas more if they feel like they had a chance to reflect or shape them.

Recommendations

1. To use the artist well means relying on your creativity. Try remembering and practicing creative acts you enjoyed as a child: drawing, acting, cooking, making music, writing. By giving yourself permission to create at all hours of the day, you give yourself permission to work with the creative force and this can help your groups align with the greater purpose in your and the other dad's lives.

2. Art starts with a vision. Your life is the greatest canvas you've got. Take some time to create a vision for your life, of which your group should play a role. Know that by claiming your creative instincts, your outlook and demeanor will reflect a level of enjoyment that people who are stuck in non-creative lives may react to with resentment. Keep your daily creative tasks aligned with the big creative vision that you've designed for your life. That way, when you receive feedback (solicited or unsolicited) from those whom you trust about your life and group, you will know that the daily creative tasks you perform are in harmony with your greater vision. Then, it is easier to maintain your courage to keep pushing ahead!

Power Question

The Artist as facilitator represents our ability to imagine and create enriching experiences for our participants. The Artist asks: How do you create value in your groups?

16 The Rascal

Affirmation

I am comfortable going beyond my comfort zone.

Description

The Rascal is an important and slightly dangerous archetype. He can provide a lightning bolt that can help people see a problem, often through a humorous or irreverent lens, or his lightning bolt of intended insight may pass too close and burn a participant. The Rascal is a rogue facilitator: his goal is the same as the other archetypes, but he is willing to engage in a wider spectrum of activities than the other archetypes. Especially for a group leader who is supposed to model empathy and compassion, the Rascal can be hard to understand.

The Rascal is a jokester who tries to cut through a participant's defenses with jokes and stories. The Rascal may use sarcasm, condescension, double entendres and other edgy language devices to convey an ignored or overlooked insight. The ultimate goal of the group is to help men grow into better fathers, co-parents and humans. Pointing out the distance between where a man says he wants to be and where he is now is one way to increase his awareness. Sometimes the bluntness of this approach is off-putting.

Benefits of Mischief

The Rascal is a no-holds-barred character. There is a type of teacher in certain mystical traditions who use what's called crazy wisdom. This teacher does outlandish, counterintuitive actions in the pursuit of enlightenment for his students—at least it can appear to be in pursuit of enlightenment for his students. But there is an element of crazy wisdom that can also seem self-serving to the teacher's ego. This is why The Rascal can be a mischievous archetype to use. When you invoke him as a facilitator there is an element of service to the group and also, maybe more than in many other archetypes, an element of aggrandizement for the facilitator. If you remain aware of this dynamic and use it consciously, The Rascal has a power that can break through many *affectations of ignorance* from your participants.

By affectations of ignorance I mean a tendency for people to pretend to be unaware of something that they really are aware of. Two reasons for this behavior are important. One, sometimes people appear ignorant of a situation because it's so common that they no longer pay attention to it, like a fish may ignore water or a human ignores air, although both are life sustaining. Two, sometimes people affect ignorance because it's a good way to get away with ill behavior.

Like the guy that claims, "I didn't think she'd be upset that I came home a few hours late." When people *pretend* to be asleep it's harder to wake them up then when they are really sleeping. The Rascal is authorized to use more dramatic means to poke through the illusions that participants spin around themselves.

Facilitator Example

I was facilitating a group at a child protection agency and one of the dads, Kevin, had been leaned on heavily by his social worker to attend the group. Kevin had a dominant personality and was none too happy about being in his words "forced" to attend the group. However, he was smart enough that by mid-way through the series he saw the new practices he was experimenting with were having a positive influence in his home.

Kevin had always been extremely strict with his two teenage boys. Social services became involved when he beat (his word) one of the boys with a belt and left marks on his arms and legs. Kevin believed children should be seen and not heard. But being in the group started him thinking that he didn't really know his boys even though they all lived in the same house. He realized he was missing something. Over several weeks he began asking them about themselves and having conversations about what they thought about music, school and friends.

It was a tentative closeness because Kevin still ran his home mostly like a drill sergeant. He put a lot of weight on being the "authority" in his home. Neither his wife nor the boys were used to him asking about their thoughts or feelings. Kevin told the men in the fathers' group that he didn't spend a lot of time with the boys because it felt awkward. He enjoyed that his sons were now being more animated around him and he knew the new way he had begun treating them had caused them to share information with him at a level he had not experienced since they were preschoolers. As a dad, he enjoyed the energy and wanted to build on it, but he was a little apprehensive.

I suggested they plan an outing where the whole family agreed on an activity and spent an afternoon hanging out together. Kevin complained the boys shut down when they spent more than a few minutes together.

The Rascal responded, "Don't worry, you have the authority to get them to open up and talk."

The other dads in the group laughed and Kevin looked chagrined. In a way, The Rascal was calling him out because although Kevin enjoyed a lot of authority in the home, ironically, he craved the closeness which his parenting style inhibited. In addition to teaching the boy's obedience, his sons had unwittingly been trained—apparently with his unspoken if not direct approval—to be frightened of and distant with him.

The Rascal, like the court jester of old, is often one who pokes fun at the powerful while maintaining his safety through an implicit agreement to help illuminate blind spots for powerful persons.

Participant Example

You are guaranteed to have a Rascal participant in every group. Your job as facilitator is to make sure he doesn't go too far beyond the comfort zone of your group members. He usually starts as the class clown but can become a demon quickly if not held to a healthy parameter. The Rascal uses humor and potentially offensive statements to make a point supporting personal growth and development. The Demon uses humor and offensive statements toward no good end. This is also a good dividing line to remember in your own use of The Rascal.

The Rascal participant will test you in the beginning of your relationship to see how much he can get away with. Nip the testing in the bud and The Rascal participant will remain a positive humorous addition to your group. Allow meanness, condescension and sarcasm to flow unabated and you create an unsafe environment for men to be vulnerable and grow. Since women are so often a lightning rod of emotions for men, it makes sense that The Rascal will often focus on the Y chromosome for his testing.

"I couldn't believe the bitch said that to me?!" exclaimed one Rascal about his "baby mama."

"R," I told him, "in this space, we refer to the people in our group and our family members respectfully."

"O yeah, my bad," he said, as he went on with his story. Just a small amount of redirection can go a long way.

Shadow

It's very important to have a good sense of how far is too far when dealing with The Rascal and to use this archetype sparingly even when you have a good handle on limits. There will be participants in your group whose limits are more conservative than yours. You want to help people move beyond their comfort zone because that's where all growth happens. But you don't want them so stretched that they stop participating in your group. For example, one Rascal technique I employ is cursing. Outside of a fathers' group, I'm okay with some swear words (okay, many swear words), but I use them sparingly during groups because: 1) I don't want people to become numb to them and 2) cursing will inevitably upset some people. But again, in pursuit of waking people up some drama is allowed.

It's very easy, though, to be misled by The Rascal and watch your group devolve into sophomoric humor which does no one any good. There should always be sophistication to your use of Rascal techniques and awareness of the overriding purpose of helping people become more compassionate and intelligent. Avoid using swear words, jokes, and double entendre just for effect. Have your purpose in mind every time you employ The Rascal.

Recommendations

1. You will run a more potent group if you are willing to use The Rascal. Unlike some archetypes, like The CEO, you can lead a good group without invoking The Rascal. And because there is some fear involved in using The Rascal, more timid facilitators will avoid its power. You can start to make use of him in simple ways with light humor that is not very threatening. As you see the quick results from teasing and joking with participants, you will become more confident in using The Rascal in appropriate situations. The Rascal is like cooking with a powerful spice; under-season at first so you don't ruin the dish and gradually add more to taste.

2. Remember that The Rascal is used in pursuit of enlightenment and liberation. Do not allow The Rascal in your own head or that of another group member to belittle group members or people who are not in the group. You may earn some laughs, but you will lose the respect of the men in your circle and undermine your credibility as a compassionate facilitator who can help lead others to the goal.

Power Question

The Rascal is a potent character who can bring a lot of light to your group, but could also burn members who are not ready for an out-of-the-box experience. So The Rascal asks:

How can you use indiscretion in a supportive way in your group?

17 The Humbled

Affirmation

Whether rising or falling, I am at peace.

Description

The Humbled is a helpful archetype. It reminds you to take your amazingness with a grain of salt because you can be knocked off the pedestal at any time. Growth gone awry results in The Humbled. Given the power generated by running a group, it's easy for a facilitator to get full of himself. You're working hard, helping men gain insights into their lives. Participants in the group and people in the community who hear about what you're doing begin looking up to you. You start to enjoy the praise, and you neglect to reflect deeply on your actions—you begin to ignore your blind spots. Your ego pushes in a dubious direction and before you know it you're in an indefensible position. Your facilitation becomes inaccurate, inauthentic, and hurtful. Fortunately, nature provides a fall from grace, a knock off the pedestal—a humbling—as an automatic quality control mechanism.

Let's say you get corralled into the position that physical discipline is always wrong. You start trying to chill out an abusive dad, but you overplay your card to make a point and say that physical discipline can get you in trouble with the law. You cherry-pick horror stories of kids who are beaten to death or scarred for life. You imply that corporal punishment is illegal in your state. It seems like you are making headway in encouraging out of control parents to not physically strike their children, but then some guy challenges you. He says spanking is encouraged in the Bible and helps kids learn discipline. What's more, he says, it's not illegal like you claim. DCF knew he was spanking his kids and they couldn't do anything because he didn't leave marks.

Everybody looks at you like, "Is that true?" The Humbled has arrived. You overstretched and got corrected. Your ego doesn't like it but it's good for the soul. That's what The Humbled represents, knocking down the false edifices that we, knowingly or unknowingly, build.

The primary lesson for The Humbled is not how to build solid structures, but how to tear down hazardous ones. It's an important lesson for a facilitator because having a huge ego is an obstacle to leadership in these small group settings. Maybe when you are speaking to hundreds of people you need to stand on a pedestal so everyone can see and hear you, but with a dozen or even two dozen guys (which is too many people a true "group," beyond 17 or so a group becomes a class because of the size), you want to be closer to the action—closer to the men and their responses and triggers. You want to be on equal footing with them and, obviously, if you set yourself physically or psychically above them, you will not be.

Humility is a virtue. When The Humbled is brought down, you are closer to your men. Humility helps to curb our tendency to egocentrism which can kill a group with the immature self-aggrandizement of a group leader: "Look at me, I'm running a group, I'm special!"

Benefits of Persistence with Awareness

It's not just the idea of "I'm running a group so I'm special," or "my relationship is all roses and no thorns so I'm special," or "my kids are all above average so I'm special;" any calcified belief system that traps you can become a vehicle for being Humbled. The important thing about The Humbled is not the specific belief that gets you in trouble; it's the acknowledgment that you are busted with a wrong belief. The goal of your facilitation is not just for the dads to learn about themselves, but for you to learn more about yourself too. If you are closed to new ideas or alternatives, you may be due for a thunderbolt that will shake things up. This is a necessary process to help you grow to the next level of facilitation.

If you feel like you know all the answers, you won't realize when that egotism is separating you from the guys in the group, or from a higher truth than you currently hold. Ego beliefs that separate you from others and cause a humbling can be based on anything, food, family, music, religion—anything you have strong feelings about. You may even be humbled due to feeling you are a great facilitator which creates a blind spot that needs correction. There are lots of ways to be humbled: you lose funding for a big project; your supervisor calls you out for some complaint she's received about you; you give bad advice to a dad in the group and he comes back upset. All these circumstances are opportunities for growth, but you have to accept that the universe may be trying to tell you something when things crash down around you. Maybe things are so hard because you are on the wrong path.

This is not to suggest you give up persistence, but develop persistence with awareness. The Humbled reminds you that a fall from Grace can be a reminder to get back in alignment. It's likely that Grace never left you; rather, you left it. And if your actions pulled you away from your path of wisdom, that's because your thoughts and attitudes pulled you away first. That usually happens because your "sticking thinking" got in the way. The Humbled is a gift in facilitating a group or for life in general because it helps you see when your hard outer shell gets too rigid and may be preventing real growth. The fall for The Humbled doesn't hurt anything but your ego. The hard shell of your limited personality is cracked and the good meat of higher awareness becomes available. We begin to relate to our authentic self on a deeper level after the fall. When used with awareness a fall from Grace sets us up for even greater success in the future. Although the fall feels scary as it is happening, it is ultimately liberating and corrective.

You can often avoid the trauma of the fall by anticipating where the cracks in your armor are. What skills are you weak in? Where are the blind spots in your agenda? By being more reflective, you can avoid some of the harsher measures that a kind Universe uses to remind you you've gotten a bit off track.

Facilitator Example

This example is unique because it occurs outside the group. However, as you'll see by the anecdote, when you are really into facilitating, *nothing* is outside the group. Everything is grist for the mill, some things more than others. After proving myself adept at running fathers' groups as a consultant for a small agency, I KNEW I had found my next ideal gig when they offered me a full-time job. I happily gave notice at my old job and took a few weeks off in between gigs. That's when I felt the hardness on my right testicle. I'd been feeling my nuts as long as I can remember and this slight change in texture felt ominous. Thinking my family young and invincible when I left my last job, I had cancelled our insurance without spending the money on COBRA in-between coverage. Since the unusual texture just appeared I decided to let it ride until I started the new gig and the insurance kicked in. Then I took myself to the doctor for the first time since high school.

A series of procedures confirmed my worst fears. I had cancer—in the organ symbolically representing my manhood. Even before pulling out the metaphysical causation list in Louise Hay's classic book *You Can Heal Your Life,* I knew the cancer was related to my new job. I had just become director of a fatherhood program. Fatherhood and manhood are fairly inseparable, and manhood and testicles are inextricably linked as well. Now, at the very inception of this dream gig, I was losing one-third of the physical representation of manhood with one unkind sweep of a scalpel.

I was so high on this new position that the cancer—in my "manhood"—knocked me for a loop. Mind you, I'm not saying that facilitating fathers' groups was the cause of my testicular cancer. You should not worry about losing a nut if you start doing this work. This has not happened to another fathers' group facilitator that I know. But for me, the testicular cancer was an incredibly humbling experience exactly at the time when I would be inclined to ego trip. Hell, I still did some of that, but losing a body part in such a vulnerable place kept me humble and able to empathize with other people's challenges a bit more. Ultimately, it made me a better facilitator and if you are open to learning from all of life's experiences, you'll find that some of the most humbling experiences can be some of your best teachers.

Participant Example

Most participants are humbled just attending the group. There are a few men in every cycle who are self-improvement junkies and see the opportunity for personal development in a fathers' program, but the vast majority sign up because something is wrong at home and either they can't figure it out or they can't face the answer. Nelson was like that. He couldn't see what good would come out of sitting in a circle with a bunch of guys talking about their lives every week.

He flat out said the first week, "I don't need this. I shouldn't be here."

But Nelson had a problem that had humbled him and it led him to our group. When one of my colleagues invited him to the group, his wife had just left him and taken their three children.

Nelson was devastated. He told us, "I'm a good dad. I don't even know why she left." He literally claimed to be clueless.

Just from his narrative, however, I had a few ideas why she left. Nelson and his wife were part of the two parents working outside the home economy. But when he and his wife came home from their day jobs, Nelson acted like he had a stay at home wife who did nothing but relax while the kids were at school. If this were the case, it *might* be cool for him to just relax all evening while she cooked dinner, helped the kids with homework and got them ready for bed. Still, even if a mom was home all day a truly involved dad would want to spend some time bonding with his children. Nelson did none of that. He acted as if earning roughly half the household income was enough to justify not contributing to the evening at home. Eventually, his wife grew tired trying to point out the obvious to him and she voted with her feet.

Nelson wasn't stupid, though. He was programmed by our culture to think that a mom should do all the heavy lifting in the house. When his wife broke the script and Nelson joined the fathers' group and started participating in the sessions, he started thinking about their roles and tasks. He learned to empathize with her. To show her he understood, he started visiting his family at his in-laws' house and helping with dinner, homework, and even chores there. After several weeks of proving himself in this manner, his wife moved back home and he continued the equitable shift in tasks. At the graduation, his wife got up and spoke about how happy she was to have a new Nelson to raise children with. This was all because he was willing to humble himself and admit maybe the ideas he was working with could be improved.

Shadow

The Humbled has a natural and appealing Shadow. It's not overpowering, it's gentle and sort of sneaky. It's false modesty. Sometimes people pretend to be The Humbled in order to impress others. Humans learn early in life that narcissism is an unpleasant trait in others. So enlightened people make a sincere effort to demonstrate empathy and good facilitators know it's an essential trait for our work. Less enlightened people fake it. In the participant example above, the father might just pretend to understand how he wife feels. He puts on the cloak of The Humbled knowing in his mind shortly after his family returns home, he will go back to expecting his wife to do all the housework in addition to her day job. This is dishonest and manipulative.

The Humbled Shadow creates an integrity challenge in the facilitator. Rather than the peace spoken of in The Humbled Affirmation, the Shadow creates a lack of peace in the facilitator. If you try and fake being The Humbled, your "small, still voice within" will let you know. You need to develop discernment to hear that voice when you catch yourself boasting about how humbled you've become. If you learn to do that you can avoid a harsher wake up call. If you don't, circumstances will transpire to teach you the lesson in a more dramatic fashion.

Recommendations

1. Remember humility. The Humbled becomes a problem when you are running fantastic groups and ignore a major blind spot. Remember the idea of CANI—Constant And Never-ending Improvement. We crash into The Humbled when we start growing too big, too fast, too strong *in the wrong direction*. So a merciful universe sends us a message to correct course! The sooner you hear and heed, the less drastic the correction.

2. The Humbled can send a jarring blow to your ego. Try your best to enjoy it when it happens. Trust in the process of growth and know that the less you resist those corrections, the less painful the transition will be. Knowing that, avoid complaints and recriminations. Embrace the change! Even if it seems hard at first.

Power Question

Tony Robbins asks a wonderful question in his *Personal Power II* series that embodies The Humbled:

What's great about this problem?

18 The Healer

Affirmation

I see the perfection in myself and others.

Description

The Healer helps people become healthy and whole. The entire fathers' program is an exercise in healing. From exploring and reconciling childhood wounds, to understanding and harmonizing emotional imbalance, to acknowledging and overcoming tension and disease in the body, all this and more are within the scope of The Healer facilitator. This archetype is crucial for fathers because as men we are taught from a young age to deny our wounds.

In his book *"Reaching Up for Manhood: Transforming the Lives of Boys in America"* Geoffrey Canada imagines how – if he had been more mature at the time – he could have better served one of the young men in his afterschool program who was bragging about not showing pain when he was hurt. "I would tell him I don't think it's right that boys are rarely taught to talk about the hurt on the outside, and almost never to talk about the pain on the inside. I'd tell him it's not always good to just pick yourself up, brush yourself off, and not make a big deal of it."

We each come to the group broken and battered: you, the facilitator, and each of the participants. We are all the walking wounded. You quickly realize how profound the healing is that takes place in every session. There is no other way to honestly describe it. Bad attitudes, physical discomfort, and mental anguish all diminish within the power of the circle. The transformation is sometimes subtle and indirect. The action of sitting down in a group and sharing with men is so simple that it's hard for participants to believe *this* is actually the cause of them feeling better. Men have such a low regard for talking and listening, we may miss what really transpired in the hours we are in the group. Often our change of heart and mind is very dramatic, but initially we ascribe the healing to something else because the group couldn't have been responsible for this, could it?

You will feel the energy change in your own being, in others, and in the group. Let's start with you. At some point, you heard someone who experienced a group talk about it and you wanted to participate. That was the first healing. You got a "contact high" from someone who participated in a fathers' group, like the non-smoker who hangs around weed heads and gets high just from smelling it. Think about why you started doing groups or reading this book. Someone convinced you that you could bring more light into the world by participating in a group. Bringing more light into the world is another way to describe a healing.

When you can help people feel better, you are a healer.

But even after you've experienced it, you may wonder, how does this healing take place? As The Healer facilitator you have a role to play in bringing it about. Paradoxically, if you get attached to making it happen, you may blow opportunities to bring the healing energy into the circle. You must recognize it is not you who does the healing. You are only a conduit of the divine energy streaming through the universe. Your intention focuses that energy on the fathers' group and allows the energy to awaken the perfection that lays dormant in every being.

To facilitate the healing, during the group you can visualize a healing bubble of light bathing each man. It's not hard to do. You have to look around the group all the time anyway. When you look at each father imagine a bright aura extending several feet beyond his physical body, engulfing his being in a divine healing light. That light will then merge at the edges with the bubble surrounding each of the other men in the circle. This will in turn extend to a circle of light which extends through each of the men and just beyond the physical perimeter of the group.

Learning more about energy or vibrational healing will certainly make The Healer archetype more powerful in your groups. You can start by simply imagining the energy body, or aura, around each participant as above. As you become more comfortable with interacting with the participants in this metaphysical manner, you can step up your game by imagining different wheels of light within the energy body. Known as *chakras* in the yoga tradition, these seven major centers along the spine are the seat of security, sexuality, willpower, love, communication, imagination, and enlightenment. Just by understanding a little bit about how the chakras operate will open many new levels of interaction between you and the men in your group.

You can actually start to assess and care for imbalances in major areas of any participant's life force by tuning into the energy circulating within his physical body. There are many different systems of healing that deal with energy in the form of nutrition, movement, prayer (thought) and more. A basic tool that transcends many of the systems, however, is correct use of the breath. Most people breathe short, shallow breaths and don't take full advantage of the power of breath to oxygenate and heal the body. Reminding participants to breathe fully and deeply, and role modeling that behavior in the group, especially during times of stress is an enormous benefit for all the men in your group.

Benefits of Affirmations

Likewise, you can assist the fathers in healing on a mental and emotional level through elevated use of thoughts and ideas. A few religious men in your group may be familiar with the idea of affirmations through their use of prayer and Scripture. New Testament examples include:

"My God meets all my needs" (from Philippians 4:19);

"God gives me strength when I am weary and increases my power when I am weak" (Isaiah 40:29); and

"God keeps me in perfect peace because I trust in Him and fix my thoughts on Him" (Isaiah 26:3).

In the Islamic tradition, ""When my servant asks you (O Muhammad) about me, (tell them) I am close to them: I listen to the prayer of each supplicant when he asks Me. Let them listen to My call and believe in Me, that they may walk in the right way" (Quran 2:186); and

"Your Lord says: "Call on Me and I will answer your call" (Quran 40:60).

All Holy Books are loaded with positive affirmations—that's what religion is based on. Helping the fathers in your group who belong to specific faith traditions find the healing affirmations in their own scripture is a great practice for The Healer. However, using thoughts to affirm health, wellness, and prosperity is not limited to the religious minded. They are available to everyone who participates in your group!

You should make a point of using affirmative language as often as possible in your own life and with your group participants. Affirmations are thoughts that use of positive ideas to guide you toward a future that is in line with who you plan to become. It feels pretty good in the present too! Some of the simplest are: I love myself; I approve of myself; I forgive myself. You affirm the qualities you want to reinforce in your psyche. I am a successful parent. I am a patient father. I am a compassionate spouse. I am a good listener. I am prosperous. I am good at making money. You can affirm the qualities you want in any area of your life.

You may be thinking it would be a lie to affirm those things because they are not true. Another way to look at it is we all have the qualities we desire to some degree. You may not be a totally patient dad yet or you may not be making the kind of money you want, but the ability to manifest those qualities are inside of you. Plus, you do have some patience and you are making some money. Focusing on what you want to expand will help you become more aware of the part of you. As you practice affirming qualities you desire, you will be able to recognize them more in yourself and others. Successful parents say affirmations to their kids all the time. Treat yourself with the same kindness. There are lots of good books and CDs on affirmations, including Deepak Chopra's *The Soul of Healing Affirmations: A –Z Guide to Reprogramming the Software of the Soul.*

As The Healer facilitator it is important for you to use affirmations abundantly with the men in your group. Whenever you get a chance tell them, "You're a successful dad!" or "You're a good listener." Or, "You're a quick study." Look for places to praise those who come to your group. Not only will you be affirming their goodness, you will be role modeling how they can build confidence in their own children by affirming positive qualities in their character.

We've addressed The Healer facilitator mostly from a spiritual or energetic level, and a mental or attitudinal level. Of course, another basic way you can practice The Healer facilitator is on the physical level. Here you can encourage healthy diet and exercise. Offering a meal is a great way to encourage and support fathers attending your group. Although offering food might be more compelling in low-income neighborhoods, even men who can more easily afford their necessities enjoy the convenience of being treated to a meal. So, in the spirit of The Healer, make sure you take the opportunity to provide food that's nutritious, delicious, and appealing. These may not be the first three qualities that spring to mind when you analyze your program's food budget. Just do the best you can for the group and make it a priority to study healthy nutrition so you can practice it more in your own life, and know ways to encourage the dads in your group to eat better as they role model good health for their children.

In terms of exercise, even though you may not have time and space (or inclination) for the participants to stretch out and practice calisthenics during your sessions, you should help people plan to incorporate movement into their daily activities. It's well known that many of us have a lifestyle that is too sedentary. As you put on The Healer facilitator hat, you want to help the fathers think of fun ways they can move their bodies during their days to promote physical fitness, blood oxygenation, and increased stamina and self-confidence.

Facilitator Example

Affirmations are very powerful. Words that others, especially those we respect, direct toward us have a big impact on the way we think of ourselves. Affirmations shared with participants inspire confidence in themselves. Especially as men we so seldom hear affirming words from other men. We joke, tease, condescend, but seldom sincerely praise other men. When I'm doing initial assessments with new group members I like to look for something positive to share with the men about themselves, even if it's simply, "I can see you really love your kids." Acknowledgment of our strengths reinforces them.

A father named Ted came into my office for an assessment. He had been in and out of prison and a drug addict. He used NA to get clean, but stopped attending because he didn't like continually giving himself the message, "I'm an addict." His own father was a career criminal and his mom sounded like she had mental health problems. Ted was living with his second wife and their two kids. He admitted his home was often in conflict and chaos and he was very motivated to change that. I was psyched that he was motivated enough to answer the call and come join the group. I told him, "You're a good man, Ted" and he looked like he wanted to cry or disavow my affirmation.

> Before he had a chance to do that, I explained: "Ted, I know you've done some stuff in your life that you're not proud of and I hear that you still lose your temper and you're not the man you ultimately want to be. But you're moving in the right direction. You're making positive change and for that I mean it when I say, 'You're a good man.' You may not want to accept that now, but I affirmed that because I

know what you focus on expands. You feed the side of you that you want to see grow. If you have to qualify it, we can at least agree that, at times, you're a good man."

Ted could agree with that.

I know that some people who work with victims of violence don't like the idea of affirming the goodness of men who have been abusive and hurtful. We need to hold those men accountable with our language.

To those men we need to say something like, "Ted, you are a good man for coming out and attending group and showing interest in changing your behavior. And there are some things you do that are scary to others and this blocks your ability to be a better man—to be the man I believe you want to become."

There are many men who will come into your circle who are addicts, or abusive or mentally ill. You have to find a way to affirm their humanity and their goodness while also holding them accountable for their negative behavior toward themselves and others. Most of the men who attend your group will be familiar with the popular stick method of behavior change. You need not abandon that entirely (figuratively). But, as The Healer facilitator you need to learn to use the carrot method of behavior change much more.

Participant Example

A wonderful example of the participant Healer happens at every fathers' group graduation. Many years ago, I got the idea to print baseball caps with the phrase "Nurturing Father" on the front. Men receive that, along with a certificate, as a gift for completing the program. The men proudly wear their caps in public as a sort of talisman and I've heard stories that wearing, or even looking at the cap, is enough to change a man's behavior.

One dad I worked with called me up after he graduated to tell me this story. He was getting really upset at his wife and they had a history of impatience and violence between them. The argument—he didn't even say what it was about and I didn't ask him—was starting to escalate. He could feel himself starting to explode and then he remembered he had on his "Nurturing Father" baseball cap. At the moment he remembered, he thought: *I can't blow up this argument with my wife. That's not what a nurturing father does.* Contrary to their whole history of arguing, he stopped it by saying he had to go out for a walk. His wife was as surprised as he was at his sudden decision to change the vibe. After he came back they started talking not only about the problem with the kids but also how they argue and how walking away for awhile gave them both a nice break. He had learned to create more healing space in their relationship by remembering what happened in the fathers' group.

Shadow

The Healer facilitator is masterful at channeling healing energy to from the Infinite Source to an intended target. In order to allow the energy to flow, be it for spiritual, mental/emotional or physical healing, The Healer facilitator has to allow himself—his ego—to get out of the way. The Shadow for The Healer is being too rigid in his expectations or desires for a particular strategy or outcome. There's an old saying that if the only tool you have is a hammer every problem looks like a nail. That's why I encourage you to expand your toolbox of healing techniques so you have different options to try in different situations.

Avoid the error of fundamentalism which promotes one course of action for all participants. People are unique. Just because a healing modality worked well for you, don't assume all the men in the group will find it valuable. State your experience and let the men choose what works for them. Be open to exploring each participant's cultural background for healing paths which are part of their family's tradition. Dads will respect you more if you are aware of some of the traditional cures that their people used whether that man is from Africa, Europe, Asia or elsewhere. Learning about various healing customs is a great way to build your cultural competency.

Many of the men who come to your group may be very skeptical of terms like "healing" or "energy work." It would be counterproductive to talk a lot about those concepts when first convening a group. And since you may not know which men have issues with this sort of language, you are better off keeping it under the radar until you build a stronger rapport and degree of trust with them. They will be more open to hearing about some of more esoteric concepts after they have experienced some of the power of the group. On the other hand, occasionally you will have a participant sign up and right away he starts talking about vibrational resonance and using other terms that let you know he's been studying metaphysics on his own. Use him as an ally to introduce the healing work to others in the circle, but don't let him pull you and others into the deep end before the group as a whole is ready.

Recommendations

1. Understand that The Healer facilitator needs to target all levels of a participant's being: physical, mental/emotional, and spiritual. Hold a vision of health and wellness for all the participants in your group; be in tune with and help them focus on whatever area of healing they feel most in need of.
2. Study a variety of healing principles and techniques beyond whatever is in your program curriculum and become competent, freely offering the fathers in your group strategies that may help them without being overly attached to them using these techniques immediately. Healing will probably be a new area of growth for many participants and your patience with the process will help.

Power Question

This macro power question underlies all the concepts you teach:
How do you help the participants in your group become healthy: physically, mentally, emotionally and spiritually?

19 The Visionary

Affirmation

I see the future and make it happen.

Description

The Visionary facilitator is one of the principal and most enduring archetypes you must employ when leading a group. I'm breaking him out here near the end of the archetypal parade so you will remember him and to emphasize that the twenty-two archetypal keys, despite the format required in a book, do not appear in convenient, linear fashion. These archetypal traits work as a hologram and any key can appear at any time as needed.

The Visionary draws upon subtle ideas. As The Visionary facilitator you call into being that which does not yet exist on the material plane. You see qualities inside yourself and the men who come to your group that are not yet manifested in physical reality. Your vision of the group and each individual's participation in it encourages the men to draw positive qualities out of themselves that have been hidden and underutilized.

The Visionary does the same for you. As you are manifesting your qualities as a speaker, Salesman, Warrior, etc., you may feel unfit, you may feel unready, you may not have gained your sea legs. But you go on because you feel these archetypes burning deep in your heart. You have seen in your mind's eye what you need to become and what the fathers in your group need to become. The primary task of The Visionary facilitator is to lay out a picture of that transformation's end result so clearly, so powerfully, and so compellingly that you and the participants in your group have no choice but to rise to the occasion.

Benefits of Dreams

So first you have an idea of what is needed in the world of parenting and relationships for an enlightened man. You understand communication and empathy and accountability and begin exercising these qualities in your own life so that you are an inspiration to the men in your group. Some who organize parenting groups believe you let the participants self-direct what they want to study and talk about. But what happens when parents don't even realize what they are missing? Certainly, you want to understand and incorporate into your program each individual participant's vision of the kind of father and partner they wish to be. But what happens when dads in your group have lost touch with the vision of who they wish to become?

As children, we all have hopes and dreams of a better, more fulfilling future. But too many of us, especially in poor communities, with inadequate resources, are trained to think small. You'll never go to college. You'll never be a legitimate entrepreneur. You'll never have a healthy relationship. After years and decades of thinking like that, it's no wonder many men are unable to visualize success.

The sad truth is that we all have some of this negative thinking and the act of running a fathers' group is a demonstration of breaking some of that pattern in your own life. It's scary to be a leader and run a group. For you to step up and role model for the dads in your group and community is a big thing. To get ten or 12 guys to come to a parenting group is no small task. Acknowledge your success with the participants in the group. Let them know this was a dream of yours which you have fulfilled with their help. Talk to them about dreams they have for themselves. Understand that success breeds greater success.

There's an old saying that "A goal is a dream with a deadline." But before you get to deadlines you need to encourage the fathers in your group to simply dream again: about the father they intend to become; about a career that excites them; about the trips they want to take, about the community they plan to live. It's important that you to do the same. The book you are holding, for example, began as a dream. Dream about who you really want to be, what you really want to do, what you really want to have and prioritize the results. Next, electrify your most important dreams by determining a realistic completion date. After that, breakdown each goal into smaller objectives until you have tasks associated with it that you can do every day!

Then do them!

Facilitator Example

I've done targeted work specifically with young fathers, but I prefer groups that are open to all types of dads. These usually end up with the majority of participants in the 25 to 40 demographic. In one of these groups I persuaded a 17-year-old dad to join us. Studies show that teen fathers are at higher risk of non-involvement with their children than fathers in their 20s and 30s. Deavon was a pretty typical high school student who happened to get his girlfriend pregnant. He lived with his parents, he didn't have a job and he was doubtful about the longevity of the relationship with his girlfriend. He did, however, want to be a father. So he started attending our group.

Deavon's mom was a single parent so he hadn't directly seen a father in his home, although his uncles did come around regularly. Since he didn't have a car and I thought the two buses he needed to take to get to our group would prevent his good intention of participating, I went to pick him up every week. Some weeks, he wasn't home at the agreed upon time and I had to leave without him. But the times we did ride together, in additional to just talking about high school stuff; we talked about his vision of the role he wanted to play in his daughter's life, how he wanted his daughter to remember him when she was grown and what he would have to do now to make that happen.

Deavon was a smart kid, but he was definitely an adolescent. After he blew me off a few times when I went to pick him up, I stopped going if he wasn't there when I called. Still, even when he missed my ride he popped up at enough sessions on his own that I didn't terminate him from the group. He did miss more sessions than I typically allow, but I gave him a pass because of his youth and because he was trying. When we talked about his future in my car or in the group, Deavon was clear about his desire to nurture and care for his daughter even when situations with the baby's mom, his own family, and his outside life threatened to derail his parenting.

Deavon hung in and made it to the group's graduation. He was the star of the evening because of his youth and his persistence. In fact, a photo I took that night seemed to capture Deavon's transition from irresponsible adolescent to engaged father. He came to the program graduation late, with his family, and took obvious joy in holding his daughter throughout the ceremony. At one moment, I looked over and saw him holding a bottle, proudly feeding his three month old daughter. I rushed over and snapped the picture. Later, looking at the photo, it seemed I had captured a vision of how Deavon saw himself as a dad.

I'm sure our confidence in him helped to clarify and strengthen his ideas of the roles he wanted to play in his daughter's life. As The Visionary facilitator, knowing and transmitting positive parenting attitudes and behaviors to the men in your group will serve to help them become better fathers and set the bar at an enlightened spot for the participants.

Participant Example

Every man comes to the group with his own vision about fatherhood. Sometimes it's buried under so much gunk that you have to help him delicately excavate it like an archaeological treasure. Others come with their eyes burned onto a target. Stan was a member of the latter group. Stan had separated from the mother of his two children because they fought "all the time" and were "bad for each other." The adult conflicts caused Stan to lose regular contact with his children. Both parents had lived a wild, party life when they were together and the mom's continuation of that behavior as a single parent brought her to the attention of the state child welfare agency who determined the kids would be better off in foster care.

After the mom's repeated failures to follow the plan that the Department of Children and Families developed for her to reunite with the children, they finally reached out to Stan. He had been missing his kids desperately and already begun to evolve beyond the man who impregnated his girlfriend four years ago. Stan committed right away to do whatever it took for him to become the custodian of his children. Hence, I got a call from him one morning saying he wanted to know how to get into my "class" because DCF had told him to do it. I prefer to call them "groups" not "classes," but anyway he came to my office a couple of days later and we connected immediately.

Stan had a clear vision that his daughter and son would come to live with him and there were no obstacles that would prevent this. He was a man on a mission. Do I need to tell you that Stan was a great group participant? Very involved in all the activities, he gave encouragement to other men in the circle and genuinely wanted to learn as much as possible about being a dad because he *knew* he'd have his kids living with him soon. With that degree of vision and commitment to it, no one was surprised when Stan turned up at group in the ninth week and announced DCF had awarded him custody!

Shadow

The Visionary Shadow is not innocuous. Because vision is based in imagination, it does cast a lighter shadow over the group. But because vision sets the direction, it can create long-term consequences that are unpleasant. You could think of vision as residing in the fourth or fifth dimension, and in the three-dimensional world that you and the group inhabit, the immediate opportunity for The Visionary Shadow to cause negative repercussions are reduced.

I'd like to think that every man who begins facilitating fathers' groups is good-hearted, noble person who generates positive, powerful images for the fathers in his group, but I know that is not be entirely true. If you are one of the fortunate ones who shares an enlightening vision, as you help group participants manifest this idea you will be amply rewarded as you see men growing closer to their family members and more in tune with their own higher self.

However, if you find yourself harboring visions for the fathers and for yourself that are mixed up with ego and power trips; visions that glorify sex or violence or control of others; if you find yourself fixated with images that taken to their logical conclusions do not support family harmony; you have a problem. Fortunately, you still have time to change this vision before it solidifies into three-dimensional reality.

Creating a vision for yourself and your group comes from your heart, maybe with help from a constructive fatherhood curriculum you are attracted to. You have the sole responsibility to decide for yourself what kind of father you want to be and the men in your group retain that same right. Your co-parents, children, and other family and friends are entitled to contribute to your vision. But ultimately it is your responsibility to dig deep in your gut and decide the type of father you want to be.

The Visionary Shadow – an image that takes you away from love and family harmony – can be activated from your own twisted dreams or it can come from other people's twisted dreams. You will be offered many opportunities to fall out of integrity by building a vision that doesn't support your highest calling. Don't do it. Follow your heart when creating the vision you will manifest or when you do achieve it, you will find it less than satisfying.

Recommendations

1. Take time to study curricula, books, and websites about fatherhood that give you ideas about the type of father you want to be and want to encourage your group participants to be. Then clarify those values and qualities you find most attractive in male parenting and incorporate them as completely as possible in your own life. When you get there, it will be easy to role model and share these essentials with other men because you live them.

2. Imagine other dads in your group (and beyond it) embodying the traits you want to bring more fully into the world. Literally see yourself and your group participants becoming better communicators, more responsible and enlightened caregivers. Talk about your vision with individual men and the group as a whole. Let people know they are part of something bigger than they are. Remember the Scriptural injunction, "Without a vision, the people perish" (from Proverbs 29:18).

Power Question

Reinforce the desire for positive change that men bring to the group by asking yourself:

What vision can I support for this man that it will cause him to transform his life?

20 The Superstar

Affirmation

Yes, I am awesome!

Description

Your job as facilitator requires you to humble yourself and put the participants first. You've got to be perceptive enough to understand the different personalities in the room. You've got to make sure you're not a ball hog on the communication team. However, there are times when, as team leader, you've got to go for glory and figuratively drive the lane for the last second slam dunk, take the all net three-pointer, or make the amazing block then run the court exuberant, pump your fist and high five your teammates. There are times when you've got to be The Superstar.

The Superstar facilitator is an expert manager of group dynamics. He's a multi-faceted, facilitating genius who shines a radiant light on others in the group with just his presence. He's confident with good reason. He trusts himself and the participants trust him. Everyone knows he's the best player on the court. He's a mentor to his teammates and encourages others to shine because his place in history is secure. He knows he cannot do it alone. The Superstar facilitator draws out the goodness in others and he makes others want to play on his team—and play well.

Benefits of Abundance

As the Superstar facilitator you always seem to be in the right place, at the right time, doing the right thing. You seem to know just the right questions to ask when recruiting dads, to understand the curriculum like you wrote it and know how to nurture the participants without smothering them. You are effusive with your love, your gambles always seem to pay off and you can interrupt a participant without him feeling cut off. You make it look easy and even your mistakes make you seem more human and a better facilitator. It's clear you work hard and your enthusiastic high-fives just add to your charm.

As The Superstar facilitator you occasionally show off, but your boasts are tongue in cheek and you don't take yourself too seriously. Great things happen around you so much, you can't stop to acknowledge every single one of them. All the archetypes work in synergy and The Superstar arrives when one or more of the other archetypes click big time. Like the other archetypes, The Superstar facilitator cannot be on stage all the time, but when he's on, he's really good and it shows!

Facilitator Example

There's an activity in the curriculum I frequently use that's focused on helping dads connect with the little boy who still lives inside themselves. It's a powerful relaxation and visualization exercise that most of men enjoy. Many guys get vivid images of themselves as young boys and, despite what went on during that time it's gratifying because the exercise is about nurturing and caring for that little boy. After the activity we go around the circle and people share what their experience was like. It's a great reflection and bonding time for the group.

This night, I was leading a group that included a man who was training to be a facilitator. He really wanted to get the experience and raised a concern at the end. After a few men spoke about how moving the activity was for them, Thomas took the floor and seemed a little disgruntled. This was early in the group cycle and we were all getting to know one another. He was obviously challenging the effectiveness of the exercise for him, and by extension subtly challenging me as facilitator. It may be significant that Thomas was also a big man, well over six feet and muscular; I'm 5'8" and kind of skinny. So people paid attention when he questioned his reaction to the activity.

> Thomas: Wait a minute. I didn't really get any image of myself of as a boy.
> Me: Well, what did you experience as we were doing the visualization?
> Thomas: Not much really, I was just trying to remember what it was like to be a boy and I couldn't remember. As you continued (describing the steps we should take to remember our little boy within), I just started feeling worried and anxious that I wasn't doing it right.
> Me: Did you feel worried and anxious a lot when you were a little boy?

From the expression that lit up his face, everyone saw the light bulb go off in Thomas's mind as I asked that question.

He looked at me with a deep expression of recognition and admitted, "Yeah, I guess I did."

So I gently said what everyone in the room was thinking by this point, "So, maybe, the activity helped you get in touch with your little boy within by reminding you of the anxiety and worry he felt during that time."

The revelation was even more apparent on Thomas's face as he acknowledged, "Yeah, I guess it did."

Then Thomas looked at me like, *Damn, that was a neat trick you just pulled off connecting those two things.* At the same time, I could see the other men in the group felt a sense of awe as they witnessed a man have a revelation about his childhood. It was important for Thomas to remember the anxiety and worry that he felt as a boy and because the other men were emotionally vulnerable at that point (from doing the exercise themselves), Thomas's experience impacted them even more strongly.

There was a collective murmur around the circle; I saw some of the other dads also looking at me like I performed some kind of magic. It was really cool. Had I not been tuned in I would have missed a great moment in facilitating. I felt like The Superstar facilitator and part of the glory came from the fact that I didn't need to belabor the point about a miracle having happened; I just moved on as though things like that happen all the time. Because they do.

Participant Example

Your job is to bring out The Superstar in all your participants. Some, however, come to the game with their skills already developed to a high level. Jimmy was one such participant. He was a successful entrepreneur and got involved in the program when one of his adolescent sons started acting up. A friend referred him to the group and when he came through another world opened up for him. He became a leader during the activities. Wanting to get as much as possible out of the group, he took the chance of becoming vulnerable in front of the other guys. In doing so, he learned a lot about his reactions to his son's behaviors and was able to tame the teenager in his house through responding differently to the boy's challenging behavior.

As we got to know one another in the group and Jimmy shared more about his life as a business owner, it became apparent that his enthusiasm for his family and his business and now the group was one of the factors in his success. He became a mentor to several guys in the group. We don't have valedictorians in the program, but if we did it was clear during the graduation that Jimmy would have been it. He gave an emotional speech that captured the zeitgeist of the group and brought the audience to its feet. As if that wasn't enough, Jimmy paid for some graduates from the program to do a weekend fatherhood retreat where we dove more deeply into skill building activities around relationship and got in some powerful nurturing time as well. You might not get a financial angel in every group, but there are always fathers who stand out in their quest to be better men, and your group is the perfect place to honor and acknowledge them.

Shadow

The Superstar has a long, deep Shadow. In fact, this is one of the most dangerous archetypes to use because of the Shadow. It is very easy to get egotistical after you run a few good groups or even a few good sessions. The transformations you see in men and accolades you receive from others can make your head big. The beauty of the true Superstar facilitator is that he does not take himself too seriously. The danger is that you will. Thoughts like, *I do this better than everyone else; all fathers need to come to my group; I have more interesting stories than anyone else in the group* are all negative projections of The Superstar.

You must be the team leader and, with effort and conviction, you will do a great job. But if you move too far out in front of your team—even if you are that "good"—you will leave them behind and lose some of your swagger. The Superstar facilitator needs to be a team player. Your Superstardom is based on the interactions with your people and if you get too lost in your own greatness, you will lose the group and end up less effective.

You need to guard against these tendencies because it is part of human nature to be egocentric. Participants will test you on this by praising you effusively. You help people in this role and they will be grateful. But recognize your interconnectedness to them. You are a superstar, but remember your mission to serve people and don't put yourself first too much or you won't be as effective in the work.

Let's be honest: this is great work and you will hit the ball out of the park on many nights, but we're still talking about a starring role with a group of about a dozen guys. You're not selling out the Palladium. Take yourself with a grain of salt.

Recommendations

1. Remember that The Superstar facilitator is the culmination of lots of hard work and successful manifesting of the other archetypes. Superstars, whether in facilitation, sports, or music work really hard behind the scenes, when the lights aren't on them. You've got to practice your basic skills to be ready when the big opportunities to score come to you. Only by connecting with the inner source of your confidence and skills, will you be able to pull the rabbit out of your hat when you're on stage at the "head" of the circle. Be patient with yourself—this doesn't happen overnight.

2. Be aware of the destructive power of your ego. Some potentially great facilitators get stuck because they play The Superstar card too often. We know you're good; you don't have to keep telling us. It's far better for someone else to sing your praises, both the verbal and non-verbal (participants are aware of your non-verbal posturing, too), then for you to toot your own horn. By all means receive it when it comes, but try not to be attached to it.

Power Question

How'd you get so good?!

21 The Judge

Affirmation

I use my power of discrimination wisely.

Description

Let's get this part of the description out of the way. Lots of people have an unnecessarily funky relationship with The Judge because of the verse from the book of Matthew where Jesus is quoted as saying, "Judge not, lest ye be judged" (Matthew 7:1). This is an important idea that's been lifted out of context and has caused a lot of pain. First, the God-man did not say, "Don't judge." He said, "Don't judge, unless you want to be judged." In fact, He immediately goes on to add that the type of judgment, fair or unfair, you render others will be rendered to you. So even if you literally interpret the Bible, you are still given parameters in how you may judge.

In other words, it's reasonable, smart, and spiritual to make judgments about people and events that happen in your group (and your life). In fact, you'd be The Fool not to, which is fine, but we're knocking on another door now. You also want participants in your group to exercise their ability to be The Judge as they evaluate your group. Feedback from your participants is extremely valuable, as is your feedback to them. There will be areas in which the participants and you will be affirmed in your competence and other areas in which you both will be encouraged to grow beyond your limitations.

This archetype operates on more than one level in his interactions with a fathers' group. On one level, The Judge constantly weaves throughout the group session informally. Before we unpack that let's focus on the more formal Judge. As The Judge facilitator you can include an assessment tool for participants to objectively evaluate their parenting attitudes and behaviors when they enter the group and again when they leave. The comparison between the two not only evaluates (i.e., judges) how much the participant learned and changed during the program, but it also evaluates how successful the program and facilitator were in helping men change. This more formally organized feedback provides data for The Scientist to track. Because of our cultural ambivalence about judging which I mentioned earlier, people refrain from considering this kind of evaluation judging, but don't let them fool ya, that's exactly what it is.

Benefits of Assessment

This kind of evaluative information helps programs get money from foundations and government sources to financially support groups. So The Judge can help you obtain cash for your group. Data equal dollars. It's also good to have a short exit survey that asks participants to rate your effectiveness as a facilitator. The exit survey should include narrative descriptions which take longer, as well as numerical ratings which are quicker to do but less illuminating. If you are interested in becoming a stronger facilitator, this feedback is like gold.

The Judge facilitator is also valuable—if you are discerning with integrity—when you offer subjective "judgments" from your heart and mind during group sessions. In fact, this is one of the primary powers of the group dynamic. People in a well run group are empathic and loving and connected enough with the other participants to care about them, yet detached and distant enough to be honest. A well run small group can cut through the bullshit of hiding honest feelings due to fear of hurting the other person. This is because, first, the structure is set up to facilitate openness and honesty, probably more than even marriage. And second, the group members don't live together so everyone becomes emotionally intimate and interdependent while at the same time maintaining a high level of independence. Judgment becomes a vehicle of expressing intimacy, interdependency and independence simultaneously.

Facilitator Example

There was a very likable brother named Jeffrey in one of the groups I facilitated. He was married with a couple of young children and a job he liked working as an insurance agent. One evening about six weeks into the program he told the group he was having some personnel problems at work. A woman in his office had accused him of sexual harassment. He was worried about keeping his job because the company took these accusations seriously. As the weeks went on Jeffrey shared details about the allegations which involved a co-worker claiming he was inappropriately propositioning her. It was a difficult situation. From all we knew, Jeffrey was an upstanding and ethical person. People in the group voiced support for him and some had their own stories of women misconstruing comments they had made.

After he had been dealing with the accusations for a few weeks, Jeffrey shared he was extra concerned because this was not the first time he was accused of harassment at this company. He told the group he felt like the current accuser heard about two earlier unproven accusations and allowed those alleged incidents to prejudice their thinking against him. This disclosure of previous harassment charges was disturbing for me and other men in the group. Jeffrey became upset when I suggested that maybe there was something he was doing that caused three separate women to complain he was sexually harassing them. He wouldn't hear it. He got upset when we were talking about it after a session and I said that even if he didn't mean to harass his co-workers, there might be something about the way he interacted with the women that caused them to feel uncomfortable.

He denied any personal responsibility for the repeated accusations and was upset when he left that night. I called him the next day and several times before the next group, but he never returned my call or returned to the group, despite more calls and a letter from me. You won't lose a participant every time you invoke The Judge, but you should be willing for participants to disagree with your judgment, maybe even to the point of leaving the group. But, at least, you will have your integrity intact.

Participant Example

In one group, a father in his late 20s was describing how his girlfriend kicked him out and he was living with his mother again. He had a pattern of moving between lovers' apartments and his mother's home.

Still, the guys in the group felt bad for him, especially when he started with that old lament, "She threw me out this week."

Sad news none of us wanted to hear. I innocently asked, maybe with a twinge of intuition, "What happened?"

He started talking about being misunderstood and mistreated. However, as he dug into his tale, it was pretty obvious he was doing the mistreating. He had stayed out late with some of his boys and had told his girlfriend he'd be home by 2:00 am.

At first, he didn't mention how late he got home until another brother in the group called out, "What time did you get home?"

His face showed some combination between a sheepish smile and a cringe when he answered, "'Round six, seven o'clock." You could hear the groans in the room.

Somebody demanded, "What happened then?"

Sensing he was losing his audience, what he had initially described as "arguing" had now been downgraded to "disagreeing." But it was too late.

"Man, you can't be arguing with a woman in her apartment when you out all night, coming home five hours late. Sheet, I'da thrown your ass out too!"

I didn't even have to play the heavy; the group itself manifested The Judge. And the powerful thing is that our friend understood. If he had not brought his situation to the group, he probably could have maintained a self-righteous attitude. If he had only spoken to his crew of like-minded brethren, he probably could have maintained his happy delusion that he had been wronged. But interacting with a well facilitated group of conscious men willing to invoke The Judge, he was influenced to change his behavior. The next week he reported to the group that he did call his girlfriend to apologize and they were talking again (although he was still living with his mom).

Shadow

The Judge is a difficult archetype to use well. The Judge as facilitator can ricochet badly if used indiscriminately. That is one reason for the biblical restraints around its use. There's a human tendency to see other people's failings as more serious than our own. During that same talk, Jesus asked, "Why do you look at the twig in your brother's eye, but you do not feel the log in your own eye?" (Matthew 7:3-5)

You should use The Judge with great diligence and restraint and only after you have built a strong bond with the men in your group. A preschool teacher taught me a song her school used to guide the teachers' interactions with the children. The chorus, "Connect before you correct" is good advice for all of us. But even after building a strong connection with a group participant, he may still be rankled at any notion that he is being "corrected."

The same applies among participants. You should use a strong guideline against "cross talk" to prevent group members from judging each other at every turn. Most of us have learned by the time we reach fatherhood that judging other people, rather than leading to gratitude and a change in their behavior, strangely, often causes them to be angry at our observations. Then they are likely to return the favor by pointing out our own shortcomings. There will be dads in the group who have not learned this lesson. You may be one of them. So, as group leader, refrain from frequently playing The Judge, especially until you connect with the men at a deeper level of trust.

Recommendations

1. Use The Judge with restraint and only after building a strong relationship with group members. Also share examples of how you have used The Judge with yourself so participants don't think you are above the need for correction.

2. Be courageous enough to use The Judge when called for. The other extreme of misuse is being fearful to hold participants accountable for anything because you think they may criticize some of your faults, drop out of the group or otherwise challenge your leadership. You do no one a favor by ignoring destructive behavior. An unintended consequence of reducing prejudice on the planet is the erroneous idea that all discrimination is wrong. Discrimination is not only making decisions based on group rather than individual consideration, but also the ability to make fine distinctions. The power to discriminate allows you to avoid that drink makes you an unsafe driver, avoid dating that person who seems abusive and to choose wisely when shopping for food.

Power Question

The Judge asks:

How do you use your power of discrimination wisely?

22 The Master

Affirmation

I am a master facilitator.

Description

The Master is in control, but he's no freak. He makes it look easy. He makes sure everyone in the group feels heard. His control is understated, not overbearing. When another participant has the floor, The Master listens intently—he is a participant, too. He reflects back what is said as clearly as a sparkling mirror shows your image in the morning. The Master makes connections between ideas that are spoken and thoughts that are intimated. He is adept at using each of the archetypes as well as understanding when a particular archetype is hazardous to the health and growth of the group.

The Master starts on time and ends on time. He recruits full groups. He nurtures the participants. He knows the curriculum like the back of his hand. He's in touch with his intuition, he defends the group, and he takes time to recharge himself. The Master has an uncanny ability to read the outcome of risky behavior; he's a great closer and creator. He is paradoxically, both The Humbled and The Superstar. He helps to heal the wounds of the men in his group and their families. He can compel participants to see their vision in his own and believe in it again. The Master shines so brightly that others feel illuminated in his presence.

Benefits of Learning

Not there yet? No worries, The Master is only one of the archetypes that you need to manifest to run a fathers' group and you may not fully resonate with his vibration until you have lots of group hours under your belt. However, you will have an inkling of him from the very first time you run a group. Obviously when you are on a learning curve, many things will go differently than how you imagined them. These are your learning opportunities. They are the bricks in The Master's edifice. Each time you stumble and fall *with awareness,* you have moved into greater harmony with The Master. Remember, these archetypes are not alien to you. Each of them is present in your psyche even before you read this book. Even if you never named them, or you call them something different, they exist in each of us.

Sometimes the darkest times and hardest periods of your facilitator training are precisely the moments that allow you to radiate more of The Master facilitator energy. The journey is both linear and circular. It will take a long time to get grounded in the attitude of The Master and you will also experience it when it's not expected. You nail a reluctant recruit with an astute observation and suddenly realize, "I'm getting good at this!" You transition from one heady topic to another less charged activity with full group accord and think, "That was easy." You find yourself more and more saying the right thing at the right time and realize that your ability to call in The Master is becoming stronger. Enjoy!

Facilitator Example

There are random moments when The Master may overtake your awareness, but he frequently appears during a graduation ceremony. The fatherhood curriculum I most often use lasts for 13 sessions. The curriculum is designed so the last session includes public time for certificate presentations and graduate comments in front of friends and families, as well as private time for graduates to say goodbye to each other in one last group separate from their families. In the private setting, each participant is told by his peers why he is liked and respected, and/or what changes were observed in him during his time in the group.

After a few graduations, I realized that separating the graduates from their families during that last session took too long. Instead, I began to incorporate this powerful activity in session 12. Then in session 13 graduates could enjoy the certificate presentations, a meal with their guests and a relaxed schmooze with their friends until we shut down the show. With this little curriculum tweak from The Scientist, The Master started appearing regularly during graduations. The hard work has been done, even during graduation week you sometimes have to shore up attendance from one or two of the more at-risk participants, but once you get all your graduates in the room they will make you proud—if you've handled your business up to then.

I could mention any graduation here, because the appreciation of the participants for the work you as facilitator have helped them do is on display big time. But I remember one graduation in particular. After the certificate ceremony, as the eating and schmoozing were reaching a conclusion, one mom walked up to The Master and said, "I don't know what you did to him, but he's changed. He spends more time with the kids and helps out around the house more. Your group really works. Thank you."

Participant Example

It's hard to recognize when a father is in The Master participant mode because the fullness of the archetype can only be experienced from the inside. There may be times when, from my perspective, a father appears to be running on all cylinders but he is feels disjointed within. This could not be considered The Master participant. So culling from my experiences participating in other groups, I would speculate that The Master participant appears for most of the dads, at least once, somewhere in the first session of a series.

There is always doubt when I agree to participate in a new group of some kind. I wonder whether the time or money I'm investing could be put to better use elsewhere. I wonder whether the group leader is competent and living in integrity. I wonder if the other participants in the group are too far ahead of or behind me. I have a lot of concerns. But always, if the group comes together there is somewhere in the first, or first couple of sessions, where I recognize, Yes, this is the right place for me. At that moment, I feel blessed and grateful I had the insight to grab this opportunity.

I believe a similar experience happens for every father who completes a fathers' group. You, as facilitator, may not see it, but at some point, sitting there in that circle, he becomes aware that The Salesman facilitator was not bullshitting. There is something here that he needs and he relaxes into the magic of being in the moment and listening to his higher self who suggested, *Go ahead, try it.*

Shadow

The true Master has no Shadow. When you spontaneously align with The Master that lives inside you, there is no danger, there is no harm. There is a self-activated safety valve in The Master facilitator that tells you to push forward or step away. So when you feel The Master archetype present, you won't ego trip over the seeming miracles that happen around you because you understand yourself as a conduit for Grace and, in that awareness, there is no Shadow.

However, inevitably, there will be moments that you are not aligned with The Master and a bit of your ego tries to pretend that you are and fakes you into an unhealthy dose of grandiosity. There will be times when you feel the absence of The Master and try to kid yourself about it, but the reality of the situation will be clear to you. Your doubt is enough. When you are aligned with The Master, there is no doubt. This is a tricky point because if there is never doubt, there's probably something wrong with you. But for healthy people who experience doubt over aspects of their facilitation and, at times, feel this overarching sense of facilitation perfection that is a sign of The Master.

So I encourage you not to be hung up about The Master Shadow because it really does not exist. If you want to worry about a Shadow, which is not advised by the way, worry about The Superstar Shadow, that's the one the most often leads to The Humbled. The very nature of The Master prevents you from using it to damage you or your group. It's perfect. When you slip into funky, erroneous thoughts, you are back to exercising some other archetype Shadow. So innocently enjoy The Master when he presents himself and keep working on integrating all the other archetypes so The Master has greater access to you.

Recommendations

1. Don't push it. This is the most subtle of the facilitation archetypes and you work on it by working on all the others. The Master above all others teaches there is a unity, a synergy, and a magic involved in facilitating groups. Even if you read this whole book and meditate on one archetype every day for a year (not a bad idea), The Master will still flower when the time is right. As I said in the introduction, this is not a linear journey. The magic and the power are in the current moment.

2. Choose your favorite two or three facilitation archetypes to concentrate on and write down the qualities you imagine go with each. Or spend some time thinking about people who manifest those particular archetypes and allow their being to inspire you. Imagine some of the other possible archetypes that could help with facilitation and consider how you can incorporate them into your group management.

Power Question

In the first half of the 20th century, there was an Indian holy man named Ramana Maharshi who lived near a mountain called Arunachala. People began visiting from all over the world to seek his knowledge. Because people are different, not all aspirants received the same guidance, but to many seekers he recommended a discipline of self-inquiry which began and ended with the seeker asking himself a question which is also apropos for The Master Facilitator. The question is:

Who am I?

Acknowledgements

To my family who laid the foundation for a successful life: Mom, Dad, Carmen, Carol; and to my family that introduced me to the "fatherhood racket:" Jasmin, Patanjali and Sakeena;

To my early friends who helped save me from a life of mediocrity: Tony Edgecombe, Kent Benjamin, James Rippy, Stone Slade, Claire Fay, Christina Johnson and Nomalanga Dalili;

To my early mentors who saw light within the clouds: Magnus "Mac" MacAuley, Chris Nteta; Fox Tree and Asoka Bandarage;

To my spiritual family who came when the time was right: Satyena Ananda, Carla Johnson, Joe Best, Jay Mulhern, Joe Cook and Angela Paige Cook, Shanti Devi Vargas, Brother Rumas, Dana Zais, Stephen Hamm, Steve Carter, Tara Murphy, Satya and Suchindra Gasko, Blair Gelbond, Shunyam De Paula Alain, Kristina Ciarmataro, Wallace and Denise Brown;

To my wonderful colleagues and friends: Sharon Shay (who first asked me to facilitate fathers' groups), Keith Williams, Alice Gomes, Denise Gonsalves, Mark Perlman, John Laing, John Badalament, John Hudson, John O'Neil, (*the Johns*), Fernando Mederos, Richard Claytor, Leonard Washington, Len Hayes, Thom Bell, Jakeece Chandler, Bruce Kantor, Kelvin McMillan, Ismail Abdurrashid, Nicole Iodice, Ermolande Jean Simon, Suzin Bartley, Jack Miller, Sarita Rogers, HFM, Rayna Charles, Tanji Donald, Marybeth Dwyer, Anitza Guadarrama-Tiernan Rob Okun and Sam Williams;

To the righteous brothers and sisters in the Nubian Writers' Group, especially Christine Vaughn, Joel Mackall, and Nicole Cleckley;

To Pamela Ogletree, CEO of Children's Services of Roxbury for hosting the fathers' group photo shoot and to all the wonderful fathers that took part;

To the Writers' Room of Boston for offering a fellowship that helped me work on this book;

To Mary Lewis, editor of *Facilitating Fathers' Groups*;

To Amma, who continually inspires.

And to each of you who have touched my heart and mind and soul.

Namaste'

About the Author

Haji Shearer has facilitated hundreds of groups for fathers. He has two decades of experience working with families. He is Director of the Fatherhood Initiative at The Children's Trust where he leads the campaign to increase father involvement in home visiting and community based programs and manages a network that supports practitioners who work with fathers. Haji founded the fathers' program at the Family Nurturing Center in Dorchester that continues to provide groups for men in Boston's urban communities and beyond. He also provided years of crisis intervention services to fathers and families involved with the child welfare system.

Haji is a Licensed Social Worker who frequently presents at family strengthening conferences. His writing has appeared in The Boston Globe, Voice Male magazine and the anthology, _Men Speak Out: Views on Gender, Sex and Power_, edited by Shira Tarrant. Haji has facilitated Men's Healing Circles, Boys to Men Rites of Passages and couples workshops. He is especially interested in seeing African-American and Latino men heal from the twin traumas of racism and patriarchy. Haji and his wife, multi-media artist, Radiant Jasmin, homebirthed their two children who are now young adults successfully pursuing their own passions.

According to the Boston Globe, he "is a phenomenally engaging man."